THE ESSENTIAL CALVINISM

J. Selden Strong

GLH Publishing
Louisville, KY

Originally published in 1909 by The Pilgrim Press.
Public domain.

Republished by GLH Publishing, 2020.

ISBN:
  Paperback 978-1-64863-033-0
  Epub 978-1-64863-034-7

CONTENTS

Preface 1

I. Traditional Calvinism 2

II. The Calvinism Of The Institutes 11

III. The Theological Sources Of The Institutes 23

IV. The Personal Equation 43

V. Applied Calvinism 50

VI. The Calvinistic Principle Of Authority 72

VII. The Elements Of Theocracy 88

VIII. The Dynamics Of Protestantism 102

Preface

It was the great good fortune of the author of this book to hear a very able lecture delivered by Dr. Abraham Kuyper of Holland while he was making a tour of America in 1898. This lecture treated of the political aspect of Calvinism, and called attention to the service which it had rendered to modern society in setting forth a governmental philosophy based on the conception of a personal, sovereign God.

The suggestion thus afforded, that Calvinism was something more than a system of theology, led to an investigation which has been carried on at intervals for a period of ten years. It would seem to be an opportune time to give to the public the results of this investigation, since this year is the four hundreth anniversary of the reformer's birth, and attention and interest are directed toward him and his work as never before.

In the first five chapters the author tells what conclusions he has come to regarding the real nature of Calvin's contribution to modern thought and progress, while the remaining chapters are given to a treatment of the present and future development of the principles of Calvinism and the Reformation.

J. S. S.
August 14, 1909.

I. Traditional Calvinism

The word "Calvinism" stands in the popular mind for a certain scheme of doctrine, rigid in outline, Puritanic in spirit, dogmatic in statement.

There is not lacking a cause for this impression. In the doctrinal history of the Calvinistic churches is found abundant evidence to justify such a conclusion. The attempt is made in creedal form to reduce the whole body of Christian truth into hard-set theological formulas, definite, exclusive. Undue emphasis is put upon certain phases of Biblical teaching with the result of minimizing some very important facts. An assumption of absolute certainty forbids freedom in belief and progress in thought; and reacts very disagreeably upon character and life. Then, too, many of the followers of Calvin exaggerated the naturally prominent features of his theology, thereby throwing the system out of balance, and in application calling attention to the formal rather than the vital elements of the Reformation. What is far worse, in this way they gave the world the impression that Calvin was a mere dogmatist, though a very masterful one, and obscured the fact that he was above all the servant of God and of man, who exerted upon his own generation a transcendent influence in behalf of progress and reform.

Owing to this misplaced emphasis there came in later times to the churches of Genevan origin an inert, lifeless orthodoxy, when the ideas of love and liberty were lost amid the fogs of speculative theology, and Christianity was considered a matter of correct belief rather than a way to live.

How very one-sided Christian thought had become, one may easily realize by referring to that extremely condensed statement of belief known as the "Five Points of Calvinism," which became widely current and was received as conveying an adequate idea of Calvin's important teachings. That this statement was purely a negative one, and was composed merely to offset the five points of the Arminian Remonstrants was a fact apparently lost sight of, or else unheeded in the earnestness of theological partisanship.

The five points of this brief creed were, by name, Particular Predestination; Limited Atonement; Natural Inability; Irresistible Grace; Perseverance of the Saints. A glance will show that these "points" are all subjects of speculative theology and philosophy, and largely outside the field of practical religion and morals.

It is extremely unfortunate for Calvinism that such an easily remembered formula was ever given to the world, seeing that in its origin it was a negation, and in its scope limited to the subjects of a certain theological controversy. Not only did it present a very limited view of Calvinism, but it also tended to perpetuate its peculiarities in an exaggerated form in the minds of those who sympathized with the Dutch Calvinists as over against the Arminians.

Moreover, the fact that today the Arminian statement of the five points finds general acceptance among Protestant churches, apparently justifies the conclusion that Arminianism was an altogether separate movement from Calvinism, and as such, took the field successfully against it; whereas the plain truth of the matter is that Arminianism was only Calvinism modified in certain particulars of speculative belief. And as historic perspective lengthens, we see Calvinist and Arminian representing the same great cause, differing from one another for awhile over the formal statement of truth. For even a brief perusal of the articles of the Arminian Remonstrants will show that there is very little variation therein from the teachings of Calvin. Indeed, it is a question if Arminius does not more truly represent Calvin than does Gomarus, for while Arminius may modify some of Calvin's positions, Gomarus throws Calvinism out of balance by emphasizing a tendency towards fatalism.

Far more representative of traditional Calvinism than the "Five Points," is the Confession of the Westminster Assembly. This is an orderly and well-proportioned statement of belief and the most complete and authoritative representation of Calvinistic theology outside of the "Institutes." This document furnishes the traditional Calvinism of the Presbyterians of Scotland, the Puritans of England and the early churches of New England. Its influence on thought and life within these limits has been wonderful. It took new form in sermons and creeds, in religious conversation, in theological teaching, in home instruction, even to a large extent in law and statute. In the thinking of the older men of the present day it is still a force to be reckoned with. And very often when men recast their religious thought and reject the old formula they take traditional Calvinism as a point of departure, a measure of comparison.

But the Westminster Confession is not pure Calvinism. It represents a development. The men who composed it were of a later generation and of a different race from Calvin and were not, even then, always in agreement among themselves. It is worthy of note in this regard that the Five Points of the Dutch Calvinists form an integral part of the Westminster Confession, and are all treated more or less extensively by the authors.

Particular Predestination is carefully treated in Chapter III, "Of God's Eternal Decree." God from all eternity decreed whatsoever comes to pass, though not so as to be the author of sin.

I. Traditional Calvinism 5

Some are ordained to everlasting life and some to everlasting death to the praise of God's grace and the praise of his justice, — the number is certain and definite.

The doctrine of Limited Atonement is presented under other names but comes by very certain implications. In Chapter VIII, "Of Christ the Mediator," we read that Christ purchased an everlasting inheritance for himself and all that the Father had given him. In Chapter X, "Of Effectual Calling," we find the statement that while all are called by the ministry of the Word only those effectually called, the elect of God, are saved; others never truly come to Christ and *cannot be saved*.

Natural Inability finds treatment in Chapter IX, "Of Free Will," where we are told that by the Fall man lost all ability of will to any spiritual good accompanying salvation. Chapter XVI, "Of Good Works," carries the thought still further by saying that works done by unregenerate men, though in accordance with the commands of God, are yet sinful; even the effort to be good on the part of one of the non-elect is made to bear evidence in favor of inherent and complete moral weakness.

The doctrine of Irresistible Grace we do not find treated specifically under that name. But something of nearly the same moment is presented in Chapter X, "Of Effectual Calling," where it is stated that only those predestined to salvation are effectually called, and that man is *altogether passive therein* till quickened by the Holy Spirit. It is wholly of God's grace. If we add to this the teaching both as to the Divine Decree and as to Moral Inability, we easily reach the conclusion of Irresistible Grace, for a spiritually impotent man, determined to salvation by the eternal decree of God, and effectually called thereto, can scarcely be thought of as capable of resisting divine grace when bestowed.

A separate though brief chapter (XVII) is given to the subject of the Perseverance of the Saints. Here it is stated that all whom God has accepted in Christ are to persevere to the end and be saved. This perseverance depends on the immutable decree of election; but this assurance of final grace does not free the subject from temporal judgment for further sins.

Having, then, found these five specific doctrines expressed in the Westminster Confession, the question naturally arises, Are they more than other subjects the gist of traditional Calvinism as exemplified in this standard?

If we were to reckon merely from the impression made upon the popular mind perhaps our question would have a ready answer in the affirmative, for these subjects have ever been the material of controversy, and so the more effectively kept before the mind. But in actual creed and teachings we shall find it otherwise. The "Five Points" do not figure largely in the Westminster Confession as a system of doctrine. They are really, except perchance the doctrine of Inability, only derivatives of one of the subjects treated in the Confession, and that not the main subject, i.e., the Divine Decree. The heavier and bulkier parts of the Confession are given to entirely different subjects.

In the general plan of doctrine in this Confession the first and foremost thing is the objective principle of the Reformation, the authority or infallibility of the Scriptures. This is the starting-point; it is the main assumption upon which all other teachings are based and out of which they attain their reality. They purport to derive their origin and proof from the Scriptures, and the rest of the Confession is intended merely to be a setting forth of that truth which God has revealed through prophet and Christ as there recorded. Particular Predestination and its historic partners must take their chances with other teachings supposed to be founded upon the Scriptures.

The first thing which the authors of the Westminster Confession seek to establish on the witness of the Scriptures is the doctrine of the Trinity. They present a strictly Athanasian teaching. There is but one true and living God who is the foundation

I. Traditional Calvinism

of all being, exercising a "sovereign dominion" over all creation. He exists in the form of a trinity of persons, Father, Son and Spirit, of the same substance, and equal in power and glory.

The whole teaching in regard to the Divine Decree which follows in the next chapter devolves upon the idea of "sovereign dominion," and is really only an attempt to explain the method under which that dominion operates. The supposed importance of this doctrine as being the central thought of Calvinism finds a limitation in the chapter upon Providence, where God is described as exercising a fatherly discipline upon men as his children. The decree is after all a father's decree, however much men may overlook this fact in the heat of religious controversy. Still the position of this statement in the Confession and its relative place in the system give it a prominent place among the leading ideas of Calvinism.

Another notable feature of the Westminster Confession, and so of traditional Calvinism, is the federal idea of the atonement; wherein Adam acts as the head of the race, and, having sinned, passes on his guilt to his posterity; wherein also Christ acts as a second head of the race and by his perfect righteousness and sacrifice purchases redemption for the elect; wherefore God pardons sin and imputes to the sinner the righteousness of Christ.

The Confession also sets forth at length the subjective principle of the Reformation, of which Luther was the chief exponent, Justification by Faith. This doctrine is set over against the Roman idea of good works, which are here regarded as of no avail, since no good works are possible without the help of the Holy Spirit. The Confession avoids the extreme form of Luther's statement; in which it is said that the sinner is justified by faith alone, and makes it clear that faith is simply the human condition for the divine bestowal of justification and that true faith must necessarily find expression in good works.

The Westminster Confession also gives the Reformation teaching as to the sacraments of the Church. Of the seven sacraments of the medieval era the Reformers suffer but two to remain, baptism and the Lord's Supper, and the objects of these are duly set forth as the seal of redemption and the symbol of divine communion. But it is worthy of note, that with however much consistency the Reformed creeds limit the number of sacraments to two, they with equal consistency give to marriage a real sacramental value, in that while it is regarded as a civil contract, it is based on the law of God and has not only social but "religious purposes."

We also find in the Confession characteristic Calvinistic teaching as to the strict observance of the Sabbath as a day of rest and worship; the distinction between the invisible and the visible Church; and the legalist presentation of the last judgment wherein God is a Judge who renders verdict for eternal reward or punishment upon all men, an act of mercy for the elect, an act of justice for the reprobate.

There is one point as to which the Westminster Confession fails to represent the traditional Calvinism even of English-speaking people, i.e., the theocratic idea of government; unless the simple declaration that the magistrate is ordained of God for the maintenance of order and peace may be construed to this effect. But such a mild statement can hardly be made to fit the thinking of such men as Knox and Melville in Scotland, of Cromwell and Milton in England, and of Winthrop and Davenport in New England. With these men the idea is not as to magistrates and laws, but of the State as an entity, administered in accordance with the divine will, and its citizens dealt with not simply as the citizens of the nation but as also citizens of the divine Kingdom. The theocratic idea may assume many forms, and it is sure to crop out in some way in the thinking and prac-

I. Traditional Calvinism

tise of Puritans and their descendants and find application in the administration of affairs of State.

Calvinism found expression in other confessions than that of the Westminster Assembly, though never so exhaustively or authoritatively. A statement called the "First Scotch Confession" was made and presented to the Scotch Parliament in 1560 by Knox and his associates. This was a strictly Calvinistic document. The theology of the Thirty-nine Articles of the Church of England is substantially Calvinistic, though in many ways it is out of harmony with the Westminster Confession. In 1658 delegates from the Congregational churches of England met at the Savoy Palace in London and issued a statement of faith, which, except in the matter of polity, was in substantial agreement with the Westminster Confession. The Congregationalists of New England in their turn adopted statements very similar to the Savoy Declaration, or else asserted their agreement with the Westminster Confession.

On the Continent traditional Calvinism took a somewhat different course. The contest between the two factions of the Dutch Calvinistic churches has already been alluded to. Besides the Five Decrees of the Synod of Dort which registered the decision of that assembly against Arminius and his followers, approval was given to a statement of faith known as the "Belgic Confession." This confession was the work of Guido de Brès, assisted by Adrien de Saravia, professor of theology in Leyden. It was revised by Francis Junius of Bourges, who had been a student under Calvin, and was printed about 1565. This confession is considered by some to be the best creedal statement of Calvinism next to the Westminster Confession. It was approved by all the synods of the Dutch churches and became their accepted statement of faith.

But this confession seems to follow an earlier one, or at least is very like it in doctrine and outline,—the Gallican Confession, adopted as the symbol of their faith by the French Protestants in their first synod at Paris in 1559. The first draft of this confession was made by Calvin himself. It was slightly modified or revised by the synod and in that form became the doctrinal formula of the Huguenots. It would scarcely serve our purpose to outline these creeds. It may be sufficient to state that they are more directly in accord with Calvin's teaching in the "Institutes" than are the Scotch and English Confessions, and follow nearly the same order of thought and have the same choice of subjects. And as compared with the Westminster Confession, while they deal largely with the same subjects, they lack that force of emphasis on certain doctrines and that careful logical arrangement which are so characteristic of the English Confession.

We may restate our conclusions in brief. Traditional Calvinism gives us as its first principle the doctrine of the infallibility of the Scriptures. It then presents us with the idea of an absolutely sovereign God who exists in the form of a trinity of persons. It presents man as morally incapable and unworthy of divine favor on account of innate and inherited depravity; but by divine and gracious decree through Christ's sacrifice and atonement for sin on the divine side, and the possession of justifying faith on the human side, a certain number of the race, called the elect, are saved from death at the last judgment.

The will of God projects itself into human society, creating the religious order called the Church, recognized as such by the possession and proclamation of gospel truth, the redeemed life of its members, the observance of the sacraments of baptism and the Lord's Supper and the keeping of the Sabbath—and being invisible the whole company of the elect of every race and age; creating also the social order called the State, which is an organization for the maintenance of peace and order, and for the carrying out of God's plan in the developing history of the world.

II. The Calvinism Of The Institutes

To one familiar only with the formulas of traditional Calvinism, the reading of the "Institutes of the Christian Religion" brings a great surprise. There is an absence of that conciseness of dogma and that sureness of statement which we naturally associate with Calvinism. Instead there is a breadth of thought, a fulness of treatment, a judicial dealing with every case which takes into account the reasoning powers of the reader, with the purpose of helping him think instead of furnishing the thought formulated and ready to be fitted into the mind. It would be difficult to find a single subject, even an insignificant one, in the two large volumes, which the author does not submit to reason, and for which he does not make an appeal to authorities in the Scriptures and among the Church Fathers.

Then, too, for all its antiquity, the Institutes is a very readable work. The style is lucid, the language pure, the use of words certain, the progress of thought is ever toward a definite end, and there is a wonderful freedom from circumlocution and meaningless phrases. It is quite free also from technical terms, and capable of being easily understood and appreciated by a mind of ordinary training and education. Indeed, one comes certainly to a conclusion that is utterly at variance with the tradition of a dogmatic Calvin,—that the book was written, not to be a final statement of theology, but simply to serve as an introduction to the study of the Scriptures and as an aid to the interpretation of them.

That this conclusion is not amiss is confirmed by the words of Calvin himself in the preface to the edition of 1559: "My design in this work has been to prepare and qualify students of theology for the reading of the divine Word, that they may have an easy introduction to it and be enabled to proceed in it without any obstruction." This characterization of the Institutes by the author himself, the fair-minded modern reader will not wish to controvert. However much he may differ from Calvin in his thinking on certain subjects, he must allow the wonderful clearness and simplicity of Calvin's theological statements.

The plan of the work is simple. Adopting the Apostles' Creed as a fundamental, four divisions are made, God the Father; Jesus the Son; the Holy Spirit; the Holy Catholic Church.

Some insertions have to be made among the subjects mentioned in the creed. In the first book, about God the Father, is brought in the subject of the authority of the Scriptures. The second book has as an introduction to the mediatorial work of Christ, a treatment of that moral degradation of man which made mediation necessary. The words, "I believe in the Holy Ghost," are elaborated to include the whole experience of the Christian life, faith, repentance, justification, works, Christian liberty, prayer, predestination and the future life. The Holy Catholic Church finds a like fulness of treatment, including after a setting forth of the nature of the true Church, a sketch of the development of the Christian Church from the apostolic times down, and statements regarding councils, church discipline, vows and sacraments. The work ends with a chapter on civil government.

It will easily be seen from this outline that the Institutes are meant to include the whole field of Christian teaching, meaning by this all the subjects of Scriptural doctrine, of developing theology and church history. They take up in print over thirteen hundred pages. It is very obvious that the "Five Points of Cal-

II. The Calvinism Of The Institutes

vinism" do not even in a condensed form represent this great body of teaching. In fact, two of them, Limited Atonement and Irresistible Grace are not found in the Institutes at all, though doubtless many would claim them to be logical inferences from statements actually made. A third, the Perseverance of the Saints, finds but a brief treatment. It is simply stated in a few lines that the elect are "beyond all danger of falling away because the intercession of the Son of God for their perseverance in piety has not been rejected." But the subject he is treating bears a different name and assumes another point of view. It is the confirmation of election which comes by the effectual calling of God; in this experience the Spirit confirms and seals in the heart of the believer the certainty of his eternal salvation. The later invented phrase scarcely describes what Calvin had in mind.[1]

The subjects of the other two articles are quite fully treated. But the statement of Particular Predestination reads very differently, taken in its proper place in the Institutes, than when it stands by itself alone and briefly and tersely expressed. In the latter case it gives an impression of fatalism. In the former it is merely the theologian's working out of the idea of sovereign dominion on the part of God, and the purpose of it is to picture God as acting and planning with a perfect wisdom and justice for each particular human being that has come and is to come into the world, and all this for the higher ends of creation. This presentation of the doctrine of predestination has its kindly side; it pictures God as in kindness rescuing many of the race from the consequences of their own sinfulness. And it is not this doctrine but another that in the last analysis arouses the repugnance of the present generation and gives to the doctrine of the eternal decree its viciousness, i.e., the third of the Five Points, Natural Inability. The idea of punishment for evil-doing

---

[1] See Book III, Ch. XXIV.

is not repugnant to the normal human mind; but punishment for evil-doing in a being who has no ability to do anything else is utterly repellent to man's reason and sense of justice. It is here that we find the real weakness of Calvin's theological system; the assertion of responsibility in a subject who has no power to meet responsibility is a complete moral contradiction. It takes away the very foundation of ethics. It is even a temptation to believe in an immoral God who makes laws for his creatures that they cannot obey, and at the same time transcends those laws himself for his own purposes.

However, this does not appear on the surface of things as a glaring inconsistency. Calvin makes out quite a case in favor of this doctrine. The Bible is effectively brought into requisition, especially the writings of Paul. The Church Fathers are made to give their contribution of opinion and evidence, while Luther and nearly all the theologians of the Reformation uphold the doctrine in opposition to the Roman doctrine of good works. It is not in any way peculiar to Calvin, but was common to the Protestant thought of his time.

It seems just to say, then, that the Five Points, made so much of in a later time, do not give a correct idea of the theological teaching of Calvin, but rather are very misleading, giving as they do a very different emphasis upon the doctrines enunciated and at the same time leaving out others of more or equal importance.

A comparison of the teaching of the Institutes with the Westminster Confession discloses a notable resemblance. In fact, it would appear that the whole body of doctrine in the confession is derivable from the Institutes, if we except some things due to the influence of Dutch thought.

Nevertheless there are some very important differences. There is, first, the fact that a brief formula and an extended treatise cannot state the same things in the same way, nor make the

II. The Calvinism Of The Institutes

same impression with the same general ideas, be the likenesses ever so close in other respects. It is still further true that the Institutes contain some important elements and qualities that are lacking in the Confession, which make them by far a better balanced statement of theology. To put it in another way, they contain methods, principles or leading ideas naturally corrective of the faults of the system.

Far more important than the particular forms that doctrine took under Calvin's treatment is the method which he used in developing doctrine. This method needs three words to describe it; it is a judicious combination of the rational, critical and historical. The subjects of theology are named, classified and arranged in a system; each subject is then stated, related to other subjects and the form of the statement is approved by an appeal to reason, to the teaching of the Scriptures and to the Church Fathers, and to the evidence which is furnished by the progress of Church history and by religious experience.

The peculiar doctrines which are commonly ascribed to Calvin are not nearly so characteristic of the man as his way of putting them. For it is well understood that these doctrines were originally derived from Augustine, but the method is Calvin's. The followers of Calvin adopted his Augustinianism, but not always his method; hence the rigidity and undeveloping character of traditional Calvinism. But though such a condition might obtain for a while, it was inevitable that sometime the method which Calvin used to express the doctrinal thought of his time, should again be used for a restatement of Christian doctrine. The free expression of thought which was characteristic of the Reformation in its early stages, might be checked for a time, but it was too nearly the real genius of that great movement to be continually restrained.

It is of the highest importance to appreciate this fact for a just valuation of Calvin's theology. It shows that real Calvinism did not need to become formal or rigid; that it had within itself a corrective force that only needed an opportunity to show itself to lead to a review of the evidence and data upon which Christian doctrine is based. Any personal peculiarity of opinion on Calvin's part, or any false emphasis that was put upon some form of Christian truth in that generation, or even any fault of judgment, is subject to correction in just that same way and by that same method by which Calvin sought with so much success to correct the erroneous teaching and practises of the Middle Ages.

Of not so great importance, but yet approaching it, is another principle set forth in the Institutes, the significance of which was lost in the succeeding generations. This was the placing above the formal authority of the Scriptures the religious consciousness as acted upon by the Holy Spirit,—a continued inspiration, not, indeed, in the sense that new revelation is given, but that it is the testimony of the Spirit to the individual mind that finally establishes the authority of the revelation already given. The truth of the Scriptures is not a thing demonstrable through reason, but it is a thing which is realizable to the spiritual mind. "It obtains the credit which it deserves with us by the testimony of the Spirit. For though it conciliates us by its internal majesty, it never seriously affects us, till it is confirmed by the Spirit in our hearts."[2]

This principle the makers of the Westminster Confession did not fail to recognize, but nevertheless such a formal idea of Scriptural inspiration came to prevail that the significance of the idea was totally obscured. So this principle, though great in potentiality, failed to become a real part of traditional Calvinism. Instead, the doctrine of verbal inspiration was carried to such an extreme as to stand in the way of freedom of thought and interpretation, and theological progress was at a standstill.

---

2   Book I, Ch. VII.

II. The Calvinism Of The Institutes

Another feature of the Institutes that is of corrective influence, is Calvin's presentation of the nature of the Christian life. A comparison is often made between the Westminster Confession and the Heidelberg Catechism to the effect that the one deals with Christian belief and the other with Christian living. Calvin's treatment of the subject of Christian living relates itself to the method of the Heidelberg Catechism. It is a noble conception of true Christian living; the doctrinaire is merged in the preacher and five chapters follow one another upon this theme.[3]

Calvin starts out with the thought that the first thing in the Christian life is "that a love of righteousness, to which we have otherwise no natural propensity, be instilled into our hearts." But granted this divine beginning, the Christian life thereafter becomes an attempt on the part of man to be like his heavenly Father.

A goal is set for man to reach, a type of perfect living given in the person of Christ, and the Christian is not one who has attained perfection, but one who is advancing toward it. "Let us every one proceed according to our small ability, and prosecute the journey we have begun. No man will be so unhappy but that every day he may make some progress, however small. Therefore let us not cease to strive that we may be incessantly advancing in the way of the Lord; nor let us despair on account of the smallness of our success; for however our success may not correspond to our wishes, yet our labor is not lost when this day surpasses the preceding one, provided that with sincere simplicity we keep our end in view and press forward to the goal, not practising self-adulation, nor indulging our evil propensities, but perpetually exerting our endeavors after increasing degrees of amelioration till we shall have arrived at a perfection of goodness, which, indeed, we seek and pursue as long as we live, and shall then attain, when divested of our

---

3   Book III, Ch. VI–X.

corporeal infirmity we shall be admitted by God into complete communion with him."

This effort to obtain perfect goodness follows along three lines of activity, which Calvin finds mentioned in Paul's letter to Titus (Titus 2:12), sobriety, righteousness and godliness. "Sobriety undoubtedly means chastity and temperance, as well as a pure and frugal use of temporal blessings, and patience under poverty. Righteousness includes all the duties of equity, that every man may receive what is his due. Godliness separates us from the pollution of the world, and by true holiness unites us to God. When these virtues are indissolubly connected, they produce absolute perfection." But the attainment of these virtues comes only by a process of self-denial, first for the glory of God, then in the service of men, through whom God would have us pay our debt to him.

In another section Calvin adds, "Moreover, that we may be not weary of doing good, which otherwise would of necessity be the case, we must add also the other character mentioned by the apostle, that 'charity suffereth long, and ... is not easily provoked.'" Very vigorously he then puts the case. "Whoever, therefore, is presented to you that needs your kind offices, you have no reason to refuse him your assistance. Say that he is a stranger; yet the Lord has impressed on him a character which ought to be familiar to you; for which reason he forbids you to despise your own flesh. Say that he is contemptible and worthless; but the Lord shows him to be one whom he has deigned to grace with his image. Say that you are obliged to him for no services; but God has made him, as it were, his substitute, to whom you acknowledge yourself to be under obligations for numerous and important benefits.... If he not only has deserved no favor, but on the contrary has provoked you with injuries and insults, even this is no reason why you should not embrace him with your affection, and perform for him the offices of love."

II. The Calvinism Of The Institutes

An important branch of self-denial is cross-bearing. The difficulties, the sorrows, the infirmities, the misfortunes of life are a discipline which the child of God undergoes that he may be taught to look to the eternal in place of the temporal, and gain patience, endurance and Christ-like character.

This view of the Christian life is completed by a most sensible treatment of the subject of the Christian use of temporal blessings. A balance is to be held between the ascetic and the indulgent use of life and the means of its support, and this balance is to be found in using things in the way and for the purpose that God intended. "It must be laid down as a principle, that the use of the gifts of God is not erroneous, when it is directed to the same end for which the Creator himself has created and appointed them for us; since he has created them for our benefit, not for our injury."

"Shall the Lord have endued the flowers with such beauty, to present itself to our eyes, with such sweetness of smell, to impress our sense of smelling; and shall it be unlawful for our eyes to be affected with the beautiful sight, or our olfactory nerves with the agreeable odor? What! has he not made such a distinction of colors as to render some more agreeable than others? Has he not given to gold and silver, to ivory and marble, a beauty which makes them more precious than other metals and stones? In a word, has he not made many things worthy of our estimation, independently of any necessary use?"

"Let us discard, then, that inhuman philosophy, which, allowing no use of the creatures but what is absolutely necessary, not only deprives us of the lawful enjoyment of the divine beneficence, but which cannot be embraced till it has despoiled man of all his senses and reduced him to a senseless block. But on the other hand, we must with equal diligence oppose the licentiousness of the flesh."

This is a forceful presentation of Christian living, and whatever philosophy of salvation may accompany it, as long as it is preached it will have strong appeal to the human heart.

One other subject deserves comment along this line. It is customary to speak of the sovereignty of God as the central theme of Calvinism. It is very true that Calvin depicts God as a sovereign ruler. But this is not all. This term very imperfectly describes the thought of Calvin. It is a criticism rather than a characterization. A large amount of sovereignty must be ascribed to God in any system of theism, and we have again to note that the difficulty here is not with the doctrine but with the slavery of the human will which apparently accentuates the force of the divine will.

It seems to the author that a truer characterization of Calvin's idea of God would be that he is the great active personality of the universe. The speculative subject of what God is, in himself, finds almost no mention in the Institutes. Even the doctrine of the Trinity is explained chiefly by Scriptural quotation and annotation. God is described to us almost altogether by his doings. He is Creator of the world, he is Preserver as well. All things take place under his knowledge and power. God is set forth as trinity, not so much essentially, as in effecting the salvation of men and in bringing about the desired course and progress of world history. God, as Calvin describes him, is not so much the All-powerful One, the All-present, the All-wise, the All-holy One, as he is the *All-active One*. The effect of such a presentation of the divine nature is to give an intense impression of God as a person, the master person in a world of lesser persons, the father spirit in the world of human spirits.

It would be hard to estimate the effect that this idea of God had upon the world of Calvin's time. It has been often asserted that the Calvinist's surety of election kept him true in the severest trials and gave to him that sturdy moral character which so

II. The Calvinism Of The Institutes

evidently impressed itself upon the history of the Netherlands, Scotland and England. Would it not be more in accord with the truth, to say that it was due to his sureness, not of himself, but of God and the triumph of God's cause? The mere fact of being assured of salvation from death, has, in itself, no incentive to action. But the surety in the Calvinist's mind that God was doing great things and had set him to do great things also gave to him an influence and power in the developing life of the time out of all proportion to his natural gifts.

Further it may be said, that if Calvin taught the divine decree he also taught the divine love. Since the former doctrine is so intimately connected with his name, it is only justice that we should remember his teaching on the other subject.

"Because the Lord will not lose in us that which is his own, he yet discovers something that his goodness may love. For notwithstanding we are sinners through our own fault, yet we are still his creatures; notwithstanding we have brought death upon ourselves, yet he had created us for life. Thus, by a pure and gratuitous love toward us, he is excited to receive us into favor. But if there is a perpetual and irreconcilable opposition between righteousness and iniquity, he cannot receive us entirely, as long as we remain sinners. Therefore, to remove all occasion of enmity, and to reconcile us completely to himself, he abolishes all our guilt, by the expiation exhibited in the death of Christ, that we, who before were polluted and impure, may appear righteous and holy in his sight. The love of God the Father therefore precedes our reconciliation in Christ; or rather it is because he first loves, that he afterwards reconciles us to himself."[4]

We discover, then, in the Institutes, four great principles or ideas, which make the work remarkable beyond its specific doctrinal teachings; a scientific method of treating and arranging

---

4   Book II, Ch. XVI.

the material of Christian doctrine; an emphasis upon the importance of a personal spiritual experience for the understanding and expression of religious truth; a most sensible, practical and vital exposition of Christian living; and the setting forth of God through a description of his doings as the supreme and all-active personality of the universe.

III. The Theological Sources Of The Institutes

When an author presents a book to the public, it is taken for granted that he has made use of a certain amount of material from other writers ancient or modern, especially if his work be in the line of history, theology or philosophy. It is likewise to be expected that the book, if it has any particular merit, contains something original and valuable contributed by the author himself, either in material, arrangement, method of treatment or philosophical standpoint. To distinguish between these two elements is often of great critical and historical value as showing the progress of some important movement, the development of some phase of doctrine, or establishing the worth and describing the work of any great leader or school.

The theological system of John Calvin, as set forth in his "Institutes of the Christian Religion," is of such historic importance as to warrant the attempt to make this distinction in its material and construction, that we may learn, if possible, to what extent he made use of other theological writings and discover, as well, wherein lay the secret of his success as a theologian and his prominence among the leaders of thought in Reformation times. It is with this purpose in view that this chapter has been prepared.

The investigation of the subject thus presented follows naturally along three lines. (1) The statements made by Calvin himself in his different writings. (2) The circumstances and events of Calvin's life as described in different documents and narrated by his biographers. (3) A comparison of the theology of the Institutes with that of the other leaders of the Reformation.

I. The Statements of Calvin

In the successive editions of the Institutes Calvin refers continually to different authorities in theology and history and makes frequent quotations from them. In the last edition, the pages are comparatively few on which there is not found at least one such reference. But it does not necessarily follow that when allusion is made to another writer, confession of indebtedness is thereby acknowledged. Every writer in theology seeks corroboration even for his peculiar tenets, and so Calvin. Nevertheless in a large number of cases it is not only apparent that he derives his material from other sources, but it is necessarily so from the nature of the acknowledgment, or the dominance of a certain method of thought, which finds expression in his theology.

This is manifestly true in regard to the constructive use which is made of the Bible. It is very extensively quoted. It is looked upon as the final and sufficient authority on all questions of doctrine. Calvin made use of it more thoroughly and consistently than any of the other Reformers. He was minutely familiar with all its parts, and wrote scholarly commentaries on most of its books. He was acquainted with the original languages in which it was written, and though he never formally undertook the work of translation, yet he helped to revise the French translation of Olivetan, and in his different writings are contained renderings in French and Latin of a large portion of it.

In the construction of his theological system all this knowledge is brought into play. In the last edition of the Institutes, all but five of the canonical books are used as sources of doctrinal material, and almost the whole teaching of the Scriptures is reproduced. The total number of quotations thus made use of is about three thousand.

III. The Theological Sources Of The Institutes

But while all the books of the canon are regarded as available for theological purposes, there are certain ones that Calvin selects, if we may judge by the frequency of quotation, as of more importance than others in the establishing of doctrine. In the first edition of the Institutes, that of 1536, the most used book is the Epistle to the Romans. In successive editions Calvin quoted more and more from the Old Testament, especially from the Psalms, which at last affords the greatest number of quotations. But the relative importance of the Epistle to the Romans is not thereby diminished, nor is there any essential doctrinal change apparent in the later editions.

The great influence of Paul on Calvin's statements of doctrine may be shown also by the proportion in which his writings as a whole are used, as compared with other portions of the Bible. Fifty per cent of the quotations from the New Testament are from Paul's epistles though they form but twenty-five per cent of its printed matter. Thirty per cent of the quotations from the whole Bible are from Paul, and in the first edition, the formative one, the proportion is thirty-five per cent. The four Gospels, which in print take up more than twice the amount of space required for Paul's writings, are yet consulted less frequently.

This dependence upon Paul is still more manifest if we take note of the doctrines most extensively treated by Calvin: the Trinity, the divine sovereignty, election, reprobation, human depravity, justification by faith, repentance. These Calvin refers directly to the statements of Paul. They are doctrines especially emphasized by him. Paul is Calvin's chief authority.

But why should a theologian who had recourse to all parts of the Scriptures be so partial to one particular writer? A further study of the Institutes furnishes at least a partial answer. Next to the Bible Calvin quotes most from the works of Augustine. Of the eighty chapters in the last edition, about sixty contain quotations from, or references to, this noted Church father, a single chapter often containing a large number. He is appealed to generally throughout the entire treatise, but it is to be noted that those portions in which the references are most frequent relate to those very same doctrines named above as being specially characteristic of the Calvinistic system of theology.

The question comes easily to mind, Is not Calvinism, then, simply a Reformation statement of Augustinianism? It has been so considered. But it must be said that Calvin does not follow Augustine slavishly. He is eclectic in his use of this source. He often quotes only to condemn, and holds every doctrinal point as subject to the Scriptures. There is much, too, in Calvin's writings that we may seek in vain for in the works of Augustine.

It is also to be considered, that while this Church father was most quoted, other men of like authority and antiquity are frequently consulted. Notable among these are Irenæus, Eusebius, Chrysostom, Origen, Cyprian, Jerome, Ambrose, Tertullian, Aquinas, Bernard and Lombard. The decrees of the great church councils are also made use of. The classical writers of heathen Rome—Virgil, Cicero, Ovid, Seneca—are made to bear witness to the truth; and the ancient philosophers Socrates, Plato and Aristotle are brought in to testify in matters relating to theology.

This list of authorities as gathered from the Institutes is remarkable for its omission of the names of the theologians of the Reformation. In other of Calvin's writings, however, he makes mention of his connection with the other Reformers.

We may gather from his letters that he entertained a high regard for Luther and his work. In a letter to him written in January 1545, he appealed to him for approval upon some of his publications. In the previous year, writing to Bullinger, he says of Luther, "Although he were to call me a devil, I should still not the less hold him in such honor that I must acknowledge him to be an illustrious servant of God." Still earlier, in a letter written to Farel from Strasburg in 1539, he is almost jubilant because

III. The Theological Sources Of The Institutes

Luther had sent greetings to him through Bucer and had said by way of compliment, "Whose books I have read with special delight." Writing to Farel in the same year he estimates Luther as greater than Zwingli.

Calvin's correspondence also reveals great respect for Martin Bucer, whose intimate friend he was. He says of him in a letter to Bullinger, written in March 1539, "Endowed with a singularly acute and remarkably clear judgment, ... no one is more desirous to keep within the simplicity of the word of God, and less given to hunt after niceties of interpretation that are quite foreign to it." Writing again to Bullinger in 1548 in defence of Bucer, who seems to have fallen under the suspicion of the Swiss Reformers, he identifies himself with Bucer on the question of the Lord's Supper and other questions with the purpose of mediating between the two parties. In the preface to this commentary on the Epistle to the Romans, Calvin ascribes great honor to Melancthon, Bullinger and Bucer for work done previously upon the same book. Also in the closing words of the introduction to his harmony of the Gospels, he says that, in the treatment of this subject, he imitates Bucer. On the other hand, Calvin seems to have used quite an authoritative tone toward his colleague. A letter written to him in February 1549 is thoroughly hortatory and didactic. It is such as a bishop might have written to an under-shepherd.

In a letter to Viret from Strasburg in May 1540, Capito and Œcolampadius are highly praised and recommended for their commentaries on Isaiah.

There remains one more to whom Calvin openly gave tribute, Melchior Wolmar his former instructor in Greek. To him he dedicated his commentary on the Second Epistle to the Corinthians, with words of praise, and thanks him personally for the start he had given him in the study of the Greek language.

We find in Calvin's own words no clear statement of indebtedness to the theologians of his own time. We turn, therefore, to his biographers, if perchance they may shed some light on this question.

II. The Statements of the Biographers

Calvin, according to his own words in the introduction to his commentary on the Psalms, did not owe his conversion to any human agency. He declares that "God himself produced the change. He instantly subdued my heart to obedience."

We may not from this assertion hastily conclude that there had been no preparation for the change that came at last so suddenly. All the historical evidence is to the contrary. While Calvin was yet a boy the Reformation doctrines came under general discussion throughout Europe, and his university course was carried on while the battle was still hot. A man in his position could not fail to realize this nor remain unaffected by it.

It seems from a historical point of view that the first man to affect Calvin's religious opinions was Erasmus. Calvin expressed as a youth a great admiration for this scholar and called him "the honor and delight of the world of letters." His first outlook upon the religious condition of the times was in likeness to Erasmus, that of the Humanist, as was true also of Melancthon and Zwingli. It was in the spirit of this school of culture that he wrote his commentary on Seneca's "De Clementia," published in April 1532. Moreover, to be a follower of Erasmus meant something more than to be a man of letters or classical scholar; it involved also a study of the Bible, in which Calvin was already proficient, and an attitude of criticism toward the existing state of affairs in the Church, together with a desire for reform. That Calvin had reached this position also follows almost necessarily from the fact that his conversion to the cause of the antipapal reformers came within a short time after the publication of the commentary on Seneca.

III. The Theological Sources Of The Institutes

Within a year or two of Calvin's conversion they were at work together in the interests of the Reformation. This was during the preparation of the first edition of the Institutes. It would appear, then, that through Olivetan, Calvin was indirectly brought into connection with the Reformation under Bucer, who was a disciple of Luther.

A more direct connection with Bucer is suggested by a letter which Calvin wrote him in September 1532 from Noyon. The object of the letter is to recommend to Bucer's care a certain French refugee who was in hard circumstances. Certain presumptions are created by this letter. It is not distinctly stated that the refugee was a Protestant, but inasmuch as he was suspected of being an Anabaptist, wrongly as we may judge by the letter, and is committed to the care of the leading Reformer of Strasburg, the implication is that he was of the Reformed faith. There is a similar presumption in regard to Calvin himself. He is evidently known to Bucer. He signs himself simply "Calvin." The inference would be that Bucer knew of him as a Protestant, else how should the recommendation be of any avail or even reasonable?

Two years later Calvin, himself a refugee, sought an asylum at Strasburg, and was welcomed by Bucer. But he soon left Strasburg and went to Basel where he finished the preparation of his Institutes. In this region he came within the circle of influence of both the Lutheran and Zwinglian Reformers and became acquainted more or less intimately with Bucer, Capito, Grynæus, Myconius and Bullinger.

We find from the biographers of Calvin that before the publication of the first edition of the Institutes he came in contact with such important Reformers as Lefèvre, Bucer and Bullinger and their associates; that he was familiar with the writings of Erasmus, and probably had read the chief works of Luther, Melancthon and Zwingli, or at least had become familiar with their respective tenets. There is no historical evidence that he was a disciple of any particular one of them.

A further investigation carries us into the field of comparative theology.

III. Calvin's Theology as Compared with that of other Reformers.

Two things are evident in regard to the Reformation sources of Calvin's theology. (1) Calvin had the teaching and experience of all the Reformers to draw from. It is most improbable that with such a wide outlook a man of his capacities would slavishly follow any one of them. He could scarcely have attained to that power and influence which made his career so extraordinary, if he had been so dependent in this regard. (2) Calvin was in the second generation of Reformers. Protestant doctrines were proclaimed in his native land long before his conversion. He was not one of the original formulators of those doctrines. The field for original work was, then, considerably narrowed for him. If we are to look for originality in Calvin's work it must be either in an improved treatment of doctrines already enunciated, in additions thereto, or their better arrangement along some dominant principle or new method.

A certain set of doctrines containing a peculiar theory of redemption is associated with the name of Calvin. Chiefly they are these: the authority of the Scriptures, a strict teaching of the Trinity, predestination, moral depravity, sacrificial atonement and justification by faith. It has already been stated that Augustine taught these doctrines in the same form and relation. There is one qualification however. The assertion that the authority of the Scriptures is supreme, while associated with the Augustinian evangelism in the teaching of the Reformers, is not strictly a part of the system though in no way out of harmony with it. Augustine asserted the authority of the Scriptures, but he also asserted the authority of the Church. For that reason the principle does not have the same relative position in his theology as with the Reformers.

But in other respects the comparison is very complete. In regard to the doctrine of the Trinity we find him stating in his "De Trinitate," "The Father, Son and Spirit are not three gods but one God"; and "are of the same substance in an indivisible equality."[5]

In the same book, speaking of sovereignty and predestination, he says, "The will of God is the first and highest cause of all corporeal appearances and motions." (Book III, Ch. iv.) And again in the "Enchiridion," "Who will be so foolish and blasphemous as to say that God cannot change the evil wills of men, whichever, whenever, wherever he chooses? But when he does it, he does it of mercy; and when he does it not, of justice he does it not." (Ch. xcviii.)

In the "Enchiridion" we also find this statement of moral depravity, "By his (Adam's) sin the whole race, of which he was the root, was corrupted in him and thereby subjected to the penalty of death, and so it happens that all who are descended from him are tainted with the original sin." (Ch. xxvi.)

Writing of the atonement in the same book, he says, "That one sin is of so heinous a character that in one man the whole human race was originally, and as one may say, radically condemned, and it cannot be pardoned and blotted out except through the one mediator between God and man, Christ Jesus, who only has had the power to be so born as not to need a second birth." (Ch. xxviii.)

In the "Enchiridion" we find this assertion in regard to justification: "But that part of the human race to which God has promised pardon, can they be restored through the merit of their own works? God forbid! For what works can a lost man perform except so far as he has been delivered from perdition?

---

5   Book I, Ch. IV.

Can they do anything by the free determination of their own will? Again I say God forbid!" (Ch. xxx.) "And lest men should arrogate to themselves the merit of their own faith, not understanding that this too is the gift of God, that same apostle (Paul) says, 'And this not of yourselves, it is the gift of God'" (Ch. xxxi.) Again he says, "God justifies the ungodly not only by remitting the evil he has done, but also by imparting love, which rejects the evil and does the good.... The ungodly are justified by the grace of God;"—i.e., from being ungodly are made righteous."

But this emphasis on justification, though it may have been suggestive to Luther as he pondered over the works of Augustine, fails considerably of expressing what the doctrine meant to him. There is a confusing of justification with sanctification; there is also a lacking of the idea which figures so largely in Luther's presentation of faith as a great spiritual experience, the human basis of justification; so also with Calvin.

But with one or two obvious exceptions the likeness between the teaching of Augustine and Calvin is very plain. In fact, some theologians have preferred to pass by Calvin, and take their starting point in Augustine for the exposition of this system of evangelical theology.

Calvin was not alone in his appeal to Augustine. All the great Reformers, and Luther more than the others, looked to Augustine for authority. There were good reasons for this. A great contest was on, first between two parties in the Roman Church, then later between hostile organizations. It was a question of right and authority. Luther and the other Reformers found in the works of Augustine teachings that fitted in with their way of thinking. As he was one of the most revered of the Latin Fathers, it was of tremendous advantage to be able to point to him and show that he centuries before had taught the very things that the Reformation theology put so much emphasis upon. The enemy was made to furnish weapons for the campaign and they were used most effectively.

Then, too, the situation in the world of theology favored such a move. Two types of thought were contesting the field before the Reformation began, and most thinkers had taken sides in sympathy with one or the other,—Augustinianism and Pelagianism. As between the two there seemed to be but one choice for the Reformer. To start a reform on the basis of Pelagianism and with the aid of Pelagians was out of the question. There was need of something more positive, more evangelistic, and this the Reformers found in the system of Augustine.

There was still another source of power in the adoption of Augustinianism. The common reference of all the Reformers to Augustine as an authority gave them a unity of thought that was of great service. Had they not had such a one to look to in the past, had they had the task of stating the truths of the gospel entirely anew at that strenuous time, the result must have been an utter confusion of religious thought, and so a lesser success for the Reformation.

Considering that Calvin became the user of these Augustinian doctrines, it will be of importance to find out, if it be possible, how he first came by them, whether directly, or through some one or more of the Reformers.

First we may note that the supreme authority of the Scriptures was asserted before the time of the Reformation by Wycliff and Huss, but the honor of formulating the doctrine for the sixteenth century rests with Erasmus. He furthermore devoted much of his time to the study of the Bible, and prepared an edition of the Greek New Testament which proved a weapon of great value to the Reformers. The authority of the Scriptures became the objective principle of the Reformation, and was reasserted in essentially the same form by Lefèvre, Zwingli, Luther and Calvin. But it was Luther who really made it a Protestant principle by offsetting with it the authority of Pope and Church, when he came in open conflict with them, and appealed to the Christian world for sympathy and help.

It is likewise true that while both Erasmus and Lefèvre had advocated the doctrine of justification by faith, it was Luther who actually placed it before the world and made it a distinct tenet of the Reformation cause. The force and power with which he did this more effectively than the others, rested not in a better understanding of the doctrinal side of the question, but in the fact of a strong personal experience of the truth expressed in the doctrine. While a monk in the Augustinian convent at Erfurt, he had been greatly troubled by the sense of personal guilt and his relief from this burden had come through some hints from an older monk, from the vicar of the Augustinian order in Germany, John of Staupitz, who was a disciple of the mystic Tauler, and from a careful study of the Epistles of Paul, whereby he had reached a spiritual state of freedom and peace. His strong insistence upon this doctrine made it the subjective principle of the Reformation.

It was through an order of John of Staupitz, that the monks in the Augustinian monasteries of Germany should study the works of their patron saint, probably, that Luther came to have a full and direct knowledge of the theological teaching of Augustine. In addition to the reverence that Luther felt for the namesake of his order, there was that in the Latin Father, his strong experience of Christianity, and his strong way of putting doctrines, that appealed to a man of Luther's nature. After his revolt from Rome, as well as before, Luther held to a strict Augustinian theology of redemption, adding thereto by conviction and experience the supreme authority of the Scriptures and justification by faith. In this form Augustinianism became an integral part of Lutheranism, and wherever Lutheran doctrines were carried there went also the Augustinian evangelism.

III. The Theological Sources Of The Institutes

It was doubtless in this form that Calvin first became acquainted with the teachings of the German Reformation. Not, as we should judge by his own words, by the reading of Luther's works, but as ideas that became prevalent and common all over Europe as representing the teachings of Luther. But it would seem that Calvin accepted the Lutheran program as a whole. This is not equivalent to saying that this was the only source of his Protestantism. We must keep in mind his knowledge of the teachings of Erasmus, Lefèvre and Wolmar while he was still a student, and that these men represented the drift toward Protestantism, though their statements were not so pronounced as those of Luther.

But the acceptance of Lutheran Augustinianism is not the most remarkable thing in the doctrinal resemblance between Calvin and Luther. Calvin acquiesced not only in what Luther projected, but also in what he rejected. Luther gave up the worship of saints, the sacrifice of the mass, the celibacy of the priesthood, the doctrine of purgatory, the authority of Church and councils, the claims of the papacy, communion in one kind and the five so-called sacraments of confirmation, penance, extreme unction, ecclesiastical orders and matrimony. With the least possible variation this is likewise the program of Calvin, and all this appears in the very first edition of the Institutes. But even this needs qualification. Independently, Zwingli, the Swiss Reformer, had come to very similar conclusions. Protestantism was a tendency of the times, in evidence all through western Europe, originating before the time of Luther and Zwingli, and only coming to an organized expression under them. Its leading ideas were not the possession of any one man or group of men.

We are led, then, to ask the question, Does Calvin resemble Luther so strikingly as to preclude the influence of other Reformers upon his thinking?

It is easy to see that Calvin is not in the same class of Reformers as Erasmus and Lefèvre. Their Protestantism was of a milder type and went no further than to plan a reform within the Church. But there are two other Reformers to whom we might look as being in a position to strongly influence Calvin — Zwingli and Bucer.

Zwingli no less than Luther insists on the sovereignty of God, but on the counter subject of moral inability there is a divergence. While he believes in the depravity of man, and cites many passages of Scripture in proof, commenting on each one in order, he does not come to any definite statement, nor does he assert man's complete moral inability. In regard to the doctrine of the Trinity also, he shows a divergence. He places a great deal of emphasis on the immanence of God, and also on the work of Christ, but he does not treat extensively the subject of the work of the Holy Spirit. He thus presents a less balanced theory of the Trinity than either Luther or Calvin.

The most notable difference is Zwingli's doctrine of the Lord's Supper. With the other Reformers he denied the fact of transubstantiation of the elements. But he goes much farther than they. It was to him an observance in the nature of a commemoration only. "The mass is not a sacrament, but a commemoration of the sacrifice offered on the cross once for all."[6]

"It is not possible to demonstrate from the Sacred Scriptures that the body and blood of Christ essentially and corporeally are partaken of in the bread and wine of the Eucharist."[7]

This is directly opposed to the teaching of Luther, and was the one difference which prevented a union of forces between the two Reformers. Luther's interpretation of the Eucharist was given the name of "consubstantiation," the idea being that the

---

6 Sixty-seven Articles. No. xviii.

7 Ten Articles of Berne. No. iv.

III. The Theological Sources Of The Institutes

real body and blood of Christ were present *with* the bread and wine.

Calvin's view of the Supper has been called a compromise between that of Luther and that of Zwingli. It does not seem such to the author. Rather it is an adaptation of Luther's. Calvin is not satisfied to think that the actual physical body and blood of Jesus are partaken of by the communicant. He insists that there is a partaking, but it is a spiritual sustenance that is afforded the communicant in the Supper. This is practically Luther's theory of consubstantiation with the substitution of the term "spiritual" for the term "corporeal." From the facts noted, then, it would seem that, as between Luther and Zwingli, Calvin sympathized more nearly with Luther and showed much more resemblance to him in the form of his religious thought.

It remains to speak of Calvin's relation to Bucer, the Strasburg Reformer. Lang asserts in his "Evangelien Martin Butzer" that the body of the Calvinistic theology was derived from Bucer. If comparison were made between Calvin and Bucer alone it would be easy to come to this conclusion. But when we consider the wealth of theological material which Calvin had at his command and was plainly familiar with,—the Scriptures, on which he wrote extensive and scholarly commentaries, Augustine and other Church Fathers, Erasmus, Lefèvre, Luther, Melancthon and Zwingli, creeds and decrees of councils, it is simply impossible to think that Calvin simply absorbed his materials from Bucer.

Even when the first edition of the Institutes was published, it was immediately accepted as greatly superior to all previous statements of Protestantism. The Romanists styled it the "Koran of the Heretics." Now Calvin had not, so far as the evidence goes, been with Bucer enough previous to the publication of this book to be greatly influenced by him. Indeed, it would appear that the Institutes were well under way before Calvin ever saw

Bucer. Further, we may remark that there is a strong suggestion of Luther in the line of thought followed, and the formal plan of the book,—the Commandments, the Apostles' Creed, the Lord's Prayer and the Sacraments—indicates that Calvin had before him Luther's smaller catechism which follows the same form. It is fair to say, however, that this arrangement might have been suggested by some other writer, as Erasmus, who uses the same subjects in his "Enchiridion." But the arrangement taken together with the progress of the thought and the tone of the doctrinal statements justify at least the suggestion expressed above.

Lang states more particularly that he has discovered Bucerian elements in the edition of 1539. This may be granted. During Calvin's exile from Geneva he spent most of his time with Bucer at Strasburg. While there he revised the Institutes. Naturally he would be influenced somewhat in his doctrinal statements by his older colleague. For example there appears in the edition of 1539 a treatment of the relation between the Old and New Testaments. This was a subject that Bucer had written upon. Also a definition of faith similar to Bucer's appears first in this edition. Again, there is expressed the idea of the continual wrestling of the flesh and the spirit, and once more, an emphasis upon the thought of God working on the heart; both of which ideas were favorite themes with Bucer. A diligent search might reveal other points of likeness. But this is very far from saying that Calvin owes his system of theology to Bucer. After all, the evidence points the other way. The absence of these distinctly Bucerian elements from the first edition of the Institutes and their presence in the edition of 1539 is unequivocal evidence against Lang's theory; for the framework of Calvin's theology is to be found in the first edition, later publications were simply enlargements of this. A likeness on the subject of predestina-

III. The Theological Sources Of The Institutes

tion is easily explained by the fact of a common reference to Augustine.

We will do well also to note some differences between Bucer and Calvin. Bucer's idea of the work of Christ presents some variety. With him Christ is the declarer and fulfiller of God's plan of salvation, and is the exalted rather than the crucified Saviour; his spiritual work is since rather than before the Resurrection. He lays also an unusual emphasis on the doctrine of the Holy Spirit. Lang calls his theology for this reason a theology of the Holy Spirit. Bucer declares that the Holy Spirit leads to knowledge, works regeneration, and guides the development of the new life; the whole spiritual activity of the soul is thus referred to the workings of the Spirit. In his mind depravity took a more positive form than with Calvin. It was not so much a moral inability as an antagonism between man and God which could only be removed by divine intervention.

Then, too, Bucer shows a more decided leaning toward Zwingli than does Calvin. His presentation of the divine sovereignty resembles Zwingli's, while his effort to combine Luther's doctrine of the Lord's Supper with the commemoration idea of Zwingli reveals a sympathy for the latter that is quite unmistakable.

We may now summarize our conclusions as follows:

(1) The authorities named by Calvin in the Institutes, the Scriptures, Augustine and other Church Fathers, creeds and decrees of councils, are the prime sources of his theology.

(2) In addition to this Calvin draws from his fellow Reformers such material as he needs to fill out his system of thought. Erasmus was the hero of his youth, and to the impulse of humanism Calvin owes the high literary quality of his writings and his first interest in the study of the Scriptures. Luther was, by Calvin's own confession, the great hero of the Reformation, and he follows him along the line of the Augustinian evange-

lism and the theory of justification by faith, also in the advocacy of specific reforms.

But for all this, Calvinism is quite distinct from Lutheranism and was looked upon by Lutherans of a later date with suspicion and even hatred, and they showed great hostility at the incoming of Calvinism into Germany. Whatever debt, then, Calvin owed to Luther it is plain that he did not follow him slavishly. It would be more correct to say that Calvin took up the work at the point to which Luther had brought it and continued it, being among the Reformers of the second generation what Luther had been among those of the first. Taking the doctrines of the Reformation as he found them, he first proceeded to formulate them; then he added some important elements of his own and built all into a compact structure; then he applied the principles so arranged and stated to the actual problems of the time. The fact that he so treated this theological material as to gain the attention of all Europe, and acquire for himself among Protestants the title of "The Theologian" is certain evidence of theological ability.

Moreover, we shall not find the real Calvinism until we subtract those elements which we know to be Augustinian or Lutheran in their origin from Calvin's great body of teaching and work. What is left after this subtraction,—Calvin's own peculiar contribution to religious life,—will then appear distinctly. But first we shall need to review the life and character of the man himself. This will be the task of the following chapter.

IV. The Personal Equation

In order to judge of the work of any man it is necessary to know the make-up of the man, his natural capacities, his environment and opportunities. A sketch of these factors in the life of Calvin is especially in order.

I

A description of the influences and forces that affected the character and destiny of Calvin before he entered upon his career as a reformer is the first thing that requires space.

The date of Calvin's conversion is under dispute, but it is accurate enough for our purpose to know that it took place towards the close of his university course, a time when the Reformation was in active progress in Germany and Switzerland. It is in the ten years previous to this event that we may look for the formative influence and events of his life.

His birth in 1509 was so placed that the news of the Reform agitation came to his knowledge at the beginning of his education, while as yet he was not expected to form definite conclusions upon such matters. We have no reason to think that, during the first of his university life, he showed any sympathy for the Reformed doctrines as proclaimed by Luther; but they could not have escaped the attention of so observant and thoughtful a man as Calvin, even in his youth. The situation of Noyon, his native town, on the northern border of France would at least ensure this. We may note the fact also, that all over western Europe this was a time of doubt and questioning, of revolt against enslaving tradition and of urgent demands for reform. This fact must have been known and appreciated by the young student.

Gerard Calvin, father of John, was a man considerably above the ordinary, though not of noble birth. His business abilities were such that they were in demand in the service of the Church. His interest in his son, who early showed remarkable powers of mind, was one of the important elements in the early life of the Reformer. Taking advantage of his social position, he obtained for his son the very best educational advantages. The plan was at first that he should enter the service of the Church. This secured to him a theological training. But in the midst of his university course it was decided that he should become a lawyer. So he received also a legal training. From his own desire he entered into the study of the humanities. He became a humanist, a follower of Erasmus. Theology, law, humanism; of these three wisdoms Calvin absorbed much, of these he was to be a teacher, out of them he was to build a magnificent career.

One more thing of great value came to him in his later student life, an enthusiasm for the study of the Bible. While at the University of Bourges he made a thorough study of the New Testament Greek under the renowned scholar, Melchior Wolmar. This, too, was to be an essential part of his equipment as a Reformer.

There were three universities among which Calvin divided his time, Paris, Orleans, Bourges. Each one of these possessed teachers of exceptional worth and great learning, the effect of whose instruction on the young scholar it is not difficult to trace. Through this elaborate instruction, through faithful study, through contact with the better class of the young men of France, he came to possess a well-rounded culture which places him with the best scholars of Europe.

IV. The Personal Equation

It would seem, then, that it was by no accident that Calvin thus early in life received so great a variety of instruction, gained so broad a culture and so wide an experience of men. If we take all this into consideration, it may not seem so strange that, when he came before the public with his first theological work, there was presented therein a complete exposition of Biblical Christianity. Granted his mental strength, the preparation for such an achievement had been adequate. Likewise his later success as a Reformer we find to have been grounded in these years of study, when with no realization of his future career, he nevertheless prepared himself for it by faithful work in those branches of study which he found it his duty to pursue.

II

Calvin has been described in all degrees of being from that of a despotic sensualist to that of a demigod. He has suffered from slander; he has suffered from praise. Friend and foe alike have made him out to be what he was not. His character is still a matter of controversy, but it is clearly just to say of him that like other men he was faulty, but also that he was freer than most men from grossness of life.

His most prominent characteristic was intellectuality. There is ample proof of this. If all we knew of him were the books he has written, the very immensity of the mental work required to produce them would assure us of this. The critical and constructive powers revealed in them evidence as well the high quality of his thinking. From the words of his contemporaries we learn also that his mental labors were intense and protracted, and were often carried on at the expense of his health. He was intellectual to a fault.

Another prominent trait was practicality. His words and deeds were always for a definite purpose. His most rhetorical sentences have an evident point. His actions are expressions of thought and aim. He showed an unusual capacity for meeting all the needs of administration, both in ecclesiastical and civil affairs, and also in the guidance of the larger reformation in the neighboring countries. His advice was often sought, not only by the government of Geneva, but also by the officials of other nations and by other leaders in political and religious life. It was sought, not because he had attained to prominence as a Reformer, but because he was able to present something of practical worth.

He was practical to the exclusion of the sentimental, the esthetic. Few words does he offer expressive of the beauties of nature or of art. The idyllic scenery of France, the grandeur of the Alps, the striking beauty of Lake Leman, the loveliness of flower and field and forest seem to pass unnoticed by this man of affairs. Granted it was so. It was enough that he raised the bare walls of the church of the Reformed. To others he could leave the fresco, the stained window, the organ loft, the arch and spire.

Still another quality was faithfulness. This he showed even in his youth. While at the universities, it is said, he often studied far into the night, and lay awake after he had retired thinking over the lessons learned during the day. The same quality was manifest during his later work. A steadfast devotion to the cause he had chosen to sustain marked even the last hours of his life. The French people are often described as facile and changeable, but though Calvin was a Frenchman such words are unthinkable of him. When we recall that the last edition of his Institutes was the same in essence as the first, we are almost inclined to wish that he might have changed a little.

Calvin was of a retiring disposition. He himself laments his natural timidity. The leadership of the Geneva Reformation was thrust upon him almost against his will; he preferred the quieter work of teacher and writer. But once feeling it to be his duty, believing that it was the will of God that he should undertake

IV. The Personal Equation

this work, his natural fearfulness is overruled by his faith in the Master's grace. He then shows a wonderful gift of public leadership and often reveals a fearless spirit.

The most common criticism that has been made of Calvin, is that he was devoid of affection, cold, cruel. There is an appearance of truth in this charge, but the latter historians defend him from the harshness of it and bring forth good evidence in support of their statements. An examination of Calvin's correspondence furnishes contradiction to the charge of unfriendliness. He clings to the friends of his youth, and writes to them in words that are expressive of the closest intimacy, almost fond, endearing. Likewise the personal affection shown him by such men as Viret, Farel, Beza, Melancthon, bears witness that his was no unresponsive nature. Indeed it would seem that this personal element of devotion was one of the great forces by which he gained such an ascendancy over the lives of his followers.

The question of cruelty is a more serious one. The death of Servetus through the agency of Calvin is an indelible blot on an otherwise fair escutcheon. We cannot justify this thing in the light of the gospel. In this Calvin stands condemned. But it is just to say, that while he desired the execution, he believed that he was doing God service. We may record to his credit also that he was opposed to the burning at the stake. Nor was he alone in upholding the death penalty for violent heretics. All the other men of his generation believed with him. Even the mild Melancthon approved of the death of Servetus.

We attempt to describe men by relating their qualities. This seems not enough. We must know them as complete personalities. If we are to understand the character of Calvin we must clothe these qualities with personality and unite them into manhood. Then our minds may picture this striking figure of the great apostle of the Reformation, smiting with the hammer of gospel truth the rotten framework of an effete religion, and fashioning anew the structure of an independent church.

III

It seems almost impossible that a single man could have written all the books that bear Calvin's name, and maintain through them all a high standard of thinking and literary art. If the study of Calvin should by any strange chance became popular, as in the case of Shakespeare, we might almost expect another Baconian theory to account for this great literary output. And yet this was only a part of the Reformer's work.

His theological work, notably the Institutes, was of such a character as to win from the leaders of the German Reformation the title of "The Theologian," and in view of the influence which his system has had in the Protestant churches generally, the title does not seem ill-deserved. In method, in clearness of statement, in comprehensiveness, his theological work was superior to all others of his time.

But the name "Theologian," even though deserved, fails to describe all the valuable work of Calvin. As a polemical writer he was most forceful. The letter to Sadoletus, changing as it did the history of Geneva, was enough of itself to warrant this assertion. The address to Francis I, found in the Institutes, is just as remarkable, while his tracts on Reformation subjects and his "Antidotes" to the decrees of the Council of Trent and to the articles of the Sorbonne are splendid specimens of polemical writing.

In the sphere of Bible commentary Calvin's work is of the best. Spurgeon called him "The Prince of Commentators." If a great preacher of the nineteenth century had so high an estimate of his work, it must have been strikingly prominent in the sixteenth.

The literary quality that appears in all of Calvin's writings, calls to mind the fact that he began his career as a humanist by

IV. The Personal Equation

the publication of a commentary on Seneca's "De Clementia." This side of his culture is not often realized, but perhaps no part of his university training shows more plainly in his writings than this. Calvin was also a teacher. In the Academy at Geneva he spent much time in giving instruction. He was a preacher, too, and nearly every Sunday, and sometimes on week days, he preached in one of the churches of the city. Still further he was a statesman. It was he that suggested the policy of the government. It was he who formulated the laws of the republic. It was under the influence of his ideals that the whole administration of public affairs was carried on. In addition to these home duties he had more or less supervision over the churches of his communion in other countries. Geneva became the center of a great religious community with Calvin as its chief. So varied and many-sided was the work of this man.

We may not in estimating the work done be satisfied with the title of "Theologian," or "Prince of Commentators." These with "Teacher," "Preacher," "Humanist," "Statesman," fail of complete description. But there is one reality that is present in all Calvin's work. There is one purpose that rules it all. There is one thought that reconciles all the diverse elements of a varied activity—the reformation of the Church of Christ. Calvin was the great apostle in modern times of a new order of human society based upon a fresh interpretation of the truth revealed in the Scriptures.

V. Applied Calvinism

The conception of Calvin as merely a theologian, or indeed as chiefly a theologian, leads to empty results. For with such an idea those who attempt to follow him are led into a formal Calvinism, while his opponents are able to say with seeming justice that he merely restated doctrines already promulgated. Both fail to understand what the Reformer really accomplished. The field of his original achievements is shut from their view.

We set forth, then, the proposition that Calvin's originality is revealed most in realms essentially distinct from doctrinal theology, and that it finds expression therein only incidentally through his interest in and devotion to the Reform movement. What Calvin would have been without the impetus of the Reformation, may be judged by the character of his commentary on Seneca's "De Clementia," and by his natural devotion to legal studies, in which he was most proficient, often occupying the professor's chair while still classed as a student. We find here, not the churchman, but the humanist; not the theologian, but the jurist. Under the impulse of the motives here discovered there could have been no Reformer. John Calvin would have been known to us as the great humanist, jurist, statesman of sixteenth century Europe, the friend of kings and princes, their learned counsellor, the advocate of conservative political progress, the devotee of letters. That this was not so, that he is known to us as the great Genevan Reformer, is due not to the natural inclination of his genius, but is one of those striking accidents of history which we can explain only by attributing it to the providence of God.

Further, we set forth the proposition that the original work of Calvin was that of construction. The materials at hand were classified, arranged, and formed into a compact whole, the organized Reformation, a reconstruction affecting every department of life and altering the current of modern history.

The Reformation shows progressively three stages: (1) The awakening of religious thought, which was characteristic of the movement before the time of Luther; (2) a moral awakening, in which Luther was the prime mover, and in which there was a demand for active reform of abuses in the churches; (3) an attempt at reconstruction, as in the latter part of the Lutheran Reformation, but more especially in subsequent developments in Geneva, France, the Netherlands and Great Britain.

The work of Calvin was principally in the third of these stages. This was his special field of effort, and one for which he was especially adapted.

The term Calvinism has become the symbol of conservatism, and has historically been applied to the theology of the more conservative churches. On account of this, people fail to see that Calvin was by nature and work a radical. It might even seem preposterous to make such a claim, but it is nevertheless true. The people of Calvin's own time realized it. His friends praised him for the wisdom of the changes which he introduced, and his enemies cursed him as an innovator, the arch-enemy of traditional religion, an iconoclast. And what his enemies said was essentially true, but was only a part of the truth; they took no account of the other side of the case, i.e., that the ruins of old things were cleared away only for the purpose of making way for a new and better structure.

There has always been a tendency to identify the Reformation with a certain set of theological dogmas. No greater mistake could possibly be made. The Augustinian evangelism had only an incidental connection with the movement, through being the most available form of evangelism. But any other form of evangelism that took into account man's dependence on divine help in order to be saved would have answered as well or better, provided it had no peculiar feature to arouse controversy. A man might be a good Catholic and hold the Augustinian theology, or on the other hand a Protestant might follow Melancthon in his trend away from strict Augustinianism and lose none of the spirit of the Reformation.

The real Reformation after all had little to do with mere doctrine. It was concerned with life, and active faith, and spiritual and moral betterment. It was a revolt against an effete order of society and an earnest effort toward a new and improved order.

When Luther nailed his famous theses on the door of the Castle church at Wittenberg, he was concerned not with correcting doctrinal statements, but with the flagrant abuses which had crept into church life, and the prime effort of all the leaders of the Reformation was to bring about a better religious condition among the people.

Calvin was in the forefront of this movement, realizing far better than Luther the real drift of the social and moral changes then taking place, and while he put much time and effort into doctrinal statement, his main purpose was to give expression and direction to the new forces that had come to birth in the Reformation.

We have already noted in another chapter three of Calvin's contributions in the field of theology—the conception of God as the All-active One, the assertion of the practical value of man's religious consciousness and a sensible and comprehensive interpretation of the Christian life. Now we may consider the nature of Calvin's attempt to put in force his ideals of social and religious life. This effort on his part aimed at nothing less than

V. Applied Calvinism

the complete reconstruction of all departments of society, according to principles founded on the truth revealed in the Scriptures. His constructive genius shows itself along four lines and gives system and motive to theology, to preaching, to church organization and to civil government.

I

We choose the term "Biblicism" to describe Calvin's principle of theologic construction. Though, as we have seen, the subject matter of his theology is largely the result of collation, we are not therefore to conclude that the Institutes show no sign of originality. To assert this would be to belittle one of the great forces of the Reformation. Rather we may say that no one book of this period did so much to establish the work of reform as did the Institutes. Immediately after the publication of this book, the author, then a young man only twenty-six years of age, sprang into prominence as one of the chief Reformers. Protestants and Romanists alike realized the significance of the event. Yet as we compare it with the teachings of the other Reformers we find but little that had not already been promulgated. In what, then, lay its strength?

Orderliness, comprehensiveness, conciseness, proportion made the Institutes a masterful achievement. Amid the chaos of doctrinal controversy, where fundamentals are so easily obscured, the mind of Calvin comprehended the full reach of the progressive thought of the time, gave it a consistent and unified expression, and placed it before the world in a brief and readable form.

But if this were all that we could say, the widespread influence that was exerted would still be imperfectly explained. Method however pure, system however complete, cannot show why so great an effect was produced by Calvinism upon all classes of people. There was resident in Calvin's theological writing a vital energy which wrought most astonishing results.

After all, the system was but the evidence of something greater. Calvin had the capacity, almost prophetic, to perceive and give expression to fundamental principles in deeds as well as in words. This capacity is revealed in the Institutes. It is not as we examine the book page by page, or study its method and system that we come to understand its greatness, but only as we can see it to be as a whole the expression of a great thought. Luther at the Diet of Worms took his stand firmly on the authority of the Scriptures. We cannot, therefore, say that this conception is original with Calvin, but he saw more clearly than anyone else the fundamental principle of Luther's position. Luther used the Bible negatively as a means of defence, a place of refuge. In addition to this, Calvin makes it a source of construction, a base of supplies, an invading force. It is this that explains the penetrating power of Calvin's teaching. His books and in particular the Institutes found their way all over Europe. They were almost literally an invading army. Everywhere they had to be treated with, they could not be ignored. They must be forcibly excluded or surrendered to as a conquering power. Even the peculiarly individual character of the Lutheran Reformation was not forceful enough to prevent an avowed devotion to Calvin in some parts of Germany.

The use of the Bible as final authority in religion was a common characteristic of the Reformers of all classes; the usages of the churches must not conflict with the Scriptures; abuses must be corrected according to their teaching. Calvin's use of the Bible goes further. For him it contains the foundation principles of human society, the law and will of God for men. With his powerful mind he tries to grasp these principles, to bring them to expression, and to apply them to the solution of moral and social problems as they confronted him in Geneva and western Europe. And with what success history tells. His power to use the Bible in this way gave him untold influence in modern history.

Before this time there had been many things that claimed authority along with the Bible. The writings of Church Fathers, the ancient creeds, the decrees of councils, the bulls of the popes, the philosophy of Aristotle, the scholastic tradition, the priesthood, all came in to limit the sphere of the Bible. All these things Calvin leaves to one side, not as one who is ignorant, or indifferent, but as one who through the inclusiveness of his view is able to perceive the proper perspective, and place the Scriptures in the central ground of religious authority. The Bible is not merely the standard, it is the source of truth.

The Institutes were the product of a scholar; they were read chiefly by scholars. In themselves they did not come before the common people. Yet not only scholars but merchants, artisans, ordinary workmen became Calvinists. Among these, system of thought was not a thing of great importance. It did not reach them nor concern them. However, the same principle that actuated the writer of the Institutes actuated them also. The Bible became for them the sum total of all good thoughts, of all true and comforting doctrine; it was the revealed will of God. They did not read the Institutes, but in the same spirit they read the Bible, and in language less pure, perhaps, but none the less vigorous, they set forth the plain teaching of the gospel. This devotion to the Bible and the exposition of its doctrine directly is specially characteristic of Calvinists. The spirit of Biblicism reigns in them. A Calvinist without his Bible is unthinkable.

The service of the German Reformers in giving the Bible to the common people, and in rendering the worship of God in the vernacular, was of inestimable value. Likewise the work of Calvin in making the Bible in the hands of the people a constructive social and religious force, was a supplemental work of no less value. The modern Protestant is often displeased at the way in which the leader of the German Reformation clung to many of the features of the Roman Church, giving up very reluctantly, article by article, the ways of medievalism. Calvin's principle, of building all from the Word of God, contrasts his Reformatory work very sharply with that of Luther, and gives a distinct character to the nations and churches that have most yielded to his influence.

II

Another feature of the vital Calvinism of the Reformation we may describe by the term "Evangelism." The word should not be limited to the sense so often given it in these later times, when attempts are made to force a revival of religious interest. It has a wider significance. On its theoretic side it is that view of Christian experience in which man is lost in himself through sin, and saved by the grace of God alone. This is characteristic of Augustinianism as opposed to Pelagianism and semi-Pelagianism. In this form it came to Calvin from the ancient theologian. He made the most possible of it. It is in his theology in a very strict form. It is an integral part of his system. Further, evangelism is not merely a soteriological theory, it is also the principle applied, it is the proclamation of the message and as well its effect on the hearer, especially if such hearing lead to salvation. Was there this full evangelism in the life of Calvinism? Eminently so. This does not appear in the common thought upon the subject though it is not unnoticed by the historian. This is easily accounted for. The external features of Calvinism have been so accentuated in sermon and creed, that the experimental side of the movement passes easily unseen. Yet to the careful historian of this period, this evangelistic activity appears as a most essential characteristic of the Reformation conducted under Genevan auspices.

Calvin himself was a most devotional man, fully consecrated to the service of Christ and intensely interested in Christ's redeeming of others. This spirit was caught by his followers,

V. Applied Calvinism

whether they had listened to him in person, or had read his works, or had been influenced indirectly by others. Calvin had a son, an only child who died in infancy. Writing of his sorrow to an old friend, he expresses himself as being comforted by the thought of his many children in the faith who looked to him as their spiritual father. This was no poetic fancy but a most vigorous reality. There were very many even in distant places who revered Calvin and looked to him for spiritual guidance. Thousands of men inspired by him set forth with their gospel message, scattering everywhere tracts from his pen, copies of the Bible, catechisms, sermons; braving danger and death that they might make known the tidings of the cross. This devotion was the expression of faith in a personal Redeemer. They were His chosen ones; they sought to do His will and were ready to follow in the path He trod.

When one recalls the Calvinistic sermon of tradition, scholastic in form, dogmatic, often abstruse, it is difficult to connect it with the straightforward, fiery preaching of the French and Dutch evangelists of Calvinistic impulse. The materials for these discourses did not consist in large measure of accusations against the papacy. They were chiefly expository sermons. The people thirsted for the Bible and for its plain interpretation, and made extraordinary efforts to attend the services of the Protestant preachers, and, many as these were, there were not enough to supply the demand. When, therefore, an evangelist came into a neighborhood, people from far and near flocked to hear him. Often several thousands were gathered together. In some little hall, a private house, or, most characteristically, in some field outside the limits of the town, the meeting took place. After the singing of a psalm, the preacher mounted a platform and read from the Scriptures. Then followed the sermon. For hours often the exposition continued, and even then the people went away still hungering for the Word. Such was the evangelism inspired by the leader of the Genevan Reformation. It was, and is, a thing peculiar to Calvinistic and related churches. In its objective realization it was a part of Calvin's work. The thought is perhaps another's; the vitalizing of the thought, the incarnating of the truth, the organization of spiritual forces belongs to the original work of John Calvin.

Besides this immediate message of evangelism, it was given another form in the work of the Genevan schools. These were a supplement to the church. Calvin had been a humanist. His devotion to Christ and the Reformation moved him to give the benefits of knowledge to others. Much of his time and strength was given to the founding and maintaining a system of schools for the republic. The Academy, established by his educational policy, became famous in teachers and pupils. Calvin himself was one of the instructors. Others who had received an education in the great French universities were invited to share in the work. It became the great educational center of Protestantism. Here it was that the beginnings of Scotch and English Calvinism were made. Many of those exiled under Queen Mary found a refuge at Geneva, and took advantage of their sojourn there to learn from Calvin the principles of his teaching and reform. In better days they returned to their native land to apply the lessons learned here.

Of as great importance were the common schools of Geneva. They were most effective in raising the standard of life and morals among the once licentious and uncultured Genevese. Noteworthy is the idea that lay back of this policy. The child should be prepared to read the Bible for himself, to read also other books of a helpful kind, and be fitted for good service as a citizen. This latter purpose was prominent in the thought of the Reformer. He often betrays in his writings a distrust of popular sovereignty. Considering the stormy scenes that were enacted in the city of his adoption, which once meant exile and at other times threatened it, or even something worse, this fact is not surprising. We must admit that nothing could be stable in public life when an uneducated people possesses the sovereignty. Wisely, then, was the foundation laid for the future greatness of Geneva, when its educational laws required the children of the city to be educated for citizenship and for the service of Christ.

It was, then, an evangelistic purpose that gave rise to this educational movement. It was the same purpose that gave rise to the early New England schools and which still leads on to the establishment of openly Christian academies and colleges. Education to the Calvinist is of little worth if it is given a selfish aim. A bread-and-butter education is not enough. He would have the soil trained to know its God and to learn devotional living.

III

Biblicism and Evangelism might be called the acquired characteristics of Calvinism. The possibility of them lay in the nature of the man who so exemplified them. But it is questionable if they would have reached any great degree of development except for the circumstance of the Reformation. Calvin was naturally a jurist. It was in the line of administration and legal construction that his success was most brilliant. In many things he depended on other Reformers or worked out their ideas and suggestions. But in the matter of the organization of the churches he solved a problem that had been a complete puzzle to Luther and Zwingli. Luther put the seal on the doctrine of Scripture authority and reasserted the evangelical teaching of Augustine, but did not have the talent to organize his church forces. This Calvin did. He was peculiarly fitted to do it.

Set at the head of the Genevan churches, it was his work to rebuild what had been destroyed, to construct upon a different plan and on a different foundation. No problem could have been more difficult. The priestly hierarchy had ruled so long that no other discipline had been thought of for upwards of a thousand years. There seemed no precedent to go by unless it were the unfortunate one, as it proved, of entire dependence on the civil power. The task was to originate a form of church government responsible to reason, appealing to men also on the side of sentiment and at the same time having the strength to maintain itself against the attacks of the papacy, and ensure its perpetuity as an identical organization. All these requirements were met in the reconstruction of the churches of Geneva. On the basis of reason they were autonomous, self-governing and self-perpetuating. Geneva had been for a long time a republic. It was reasonable and fitting that its churches should be governed in a similar way. The changing of sentiment was far more difficult of accomplishment. When a people for centuries have been attached to the same religious forms, methods of expression and customs of worship, it is a hard thing to change their practises. The mind may be convinced, but the heart longs for the old ways. Yet in this appeal to sentiment Calvin succeeded. For the old ideas and customs he introduced new ones; the old forms he replaced with others more fitting.

His work in this respect bears evidence of antagonism to Rome. It could hardly have been otherwise. But it illustrates none the less the keen and discriminating mind of the Reformer. The Romanist grounded his authority in the Church. Its doctrine was the truth, its message the gospel. Against this conception was placed the Bible as the inspired source of authority to which Church and council must conform. Against the doctrine of the apostolic priesthood was set the doctrine of the priesthood of all believers. Against the claim of catholicity in the Roman Church was brought forward the doctrine of the invisible Catholic Church of which the visible churches are the expression. Instead of a visible ruler of the Church, as the bishop of Rome, Christ is made the real though invisible head. The visible Church is regarded as the true expression of the invisible

V. Applied Calvinism

when it sustains public worship, administers the sacraments, furnishes the preaching of the pure Word of God and maintains spiritual discipline.

This presentation of the Church was so fitted to the needs of the time as to completely drive out the old Church ideas in Reformed communities. The reverence for the Roman priesthood disappeared and with it all the practises that were connected with it.

Calvin looks to the New Testament for suggestions as to the government of the Church, and as far as possible he carries out the practises and methods applied in apostolic times. But for all this, it must be said that the ecclesiastical government and discipline of the churches of Geneva bears plainly the stamp of his peculiar genius. There is much therein that comes of his knowledge of law and the principles of administration. The scheme is more elaborate than a simple study of the Bible would warrant. The needs of this particular community are considered, and some things have only a local application.

The form of church government at Geneva was in most respects like that of the Presbyterian churches of the present day. The officers were the pastors, teachers, lay elders and deacons. These were connected with particular churches. Unity was effected by the institution of two representative bodies, the Venerable Company, clerical in its make-up, and the Consistory, a mixed body of clergymen and laymen. It was Calvin's purpose to add to these still another assembly, the synod, a superior administrative body, in order that the organization of the churches might form a complete system. In this he was prevented by the action of the civil authorities.

The ecclesiastical discipline at Geneva was strict and elaborate, and followed out Biblical suggestions. It proved to be a very important element in Calvinism. There were three steps in the treatment of refractory members, based on the words of Jesus in Matthew 18:15–17—private admonition, admonition before witnesses, and exclusion from the Lord's table. Calvin sought to have all this included in the jurisdiction of the Church. But in the matter of excommunication the civil authorities insisted on having a veto power. Nevertheless this system of discipline became famous and passed itself on into history as a vital force.

So the great thing was done. There was avoided on the one side the enervating subjection to the civil power which characterized the Lutheran churches, and on the other side the fatal error of claiming authority in civil jurisdiction. Calvin's idea was that of an independent church and an independent state government, but both administered in sympathy and supplementing each other. The historic importance of this achievement is inestimable. There was built up a veritable church-republic on final principles. The church membership was the foundation of the structure, then came the officers of the church, then the representative assemblies. It was one of the strongest forms of government ever devised, and proved itself so in more than one country. There was no need of connection with the state, as was the case at Geneva. A body of Christian believers could make a beginning anywhere, without the help, or even without reference to, any outside authority and build up church, presbytery, synod, general assembly into a strong and permanent organization. This was done more than once and in each case the new body was of the strongest and formed an essential part of the nation's activities.

The churches of Geneva could not strictly be termed free churches. They were too much under the supervision of the state authorities. This was not Calvin's doing, it was in spite of his wishes and plans. But the impetus toward freedom in church affairs was so great even under these conditions, the principle of autonomy was so plainly asserted, that we can justly say that Calvin was the father of the free church.

IV

The Reformed churches, organized as they were in the relation of a republic, contained in themselves the suggestion of free government in civil affairs, and would inevitably lead up to that question sooner or later. But Calvin did not leave the suggestion to be worked out by others. He himself in his written works and in actual life has expressed his ideas of government. This feature of Calvinism stands out very prominently. Calvin was above all a statesman, a politician if you will. It does not avail to say that he never held any civil office or took any formal part in the administration of the government. He was the recognized leader of the theocratic party at Geneva. He had a wonderful power over his constituency. The government of the city was remodeled and administered in accordance with his ideas. The code of laws in use was almost directly from his pen. His advice was asked in all important affairs of state and was usually followed. It is hardly too much to say that no man ever impressed his personality upon the life of a people more than did Calvin upon that of the Genevese. As to office, he could be called at most only head pastor, but in effect he was the ruler, by the force of his personality and by the fulness of his political wisdom, both in Church and State. No king ever realized his plans more completely, or more thoroughly attained his purpose. And yet he never took weapon into his hand nor commanded soldiery; never made show of his power nor coerced his parliament. Whatever changes were made had to be passed by vote of the general assembly of the people. His was purely a moral supremacy.

In the second volume of the Institutes is a chapter on civil government in which Calvin gives his political theory. It is of the class that is termed theocratic government administered from the religious point of view. This scheme, like that of his system of church government, looks to the Bible for its authority, and like it also is a pure product of his genius.

All government is of God. The ruler is the agent of God appointed to hold power over the community or nation. He is responsible to God, who will deal with him as with a steward. The people are to obey the ruler implicitly, for his authority is of God. But obedience to God is supreme, so the suggestion is made that in case of very oppressive tyranny, the overthrow of the existing government is right, provided God has chosen some one as his agent for the purpose.

The functions of the government are given as the establishment of true worship, the upholding of sound doctrine, the maintenance of public order, defence of the community, involving the right of war, and taxation.

Law finds its basis in the moral law of God as seen in the Bible and in the life of the nations. Its purpose is governmental. It expresses the will of God for the community and the individual. No distinction is made in the execution of the punishment between civil and religious offences. Both are against God and both are to be punished by the magistrate, who is the agent of God.

In the Bible Calvin finds no authoritative preference as to the form of government—democratic, aristocratic or monarchic. But the trend of his thought and the impulse of his work is toward free government.

This was no idle theory. The principles here described were put into actual practise in the city of Geneva. Reform there was not confined to the elevating of the morals of the people or the establishment of a New Testament church. It included also in reconstruction of the political order not less complete and lasting than that in the religious life.

Geneva had been a republic for a long time when Calvin came there. But it was in a rather loose form. Under Calvin some changes were made in form, but the greatest changes were in method of administration. The theocratic idea seeks an actual

V. Applied Calvinism

realization. The subjects of the State are regarded as the subjects of God and their acts are passed upon from that point of view.

The laws formulated by Calvin were a complete code for the administration of public affairs down to the minutest detail. Regulations were made as to behavior, dress, church attendance, education, amusements and luxuries, besides matters that ordinarily enter into enactments of the kind. These laws were maintained in force for many years until the character of the Genevese was completely altered.

In other lands than Switzerland Calvinism came to be a transforming power in a political way through the teaching of Calvin, through the example of Geneva, and indirectly through the churches.

The history of the Netherlands in the sixteenth and seventeenth centuries is chiefly the history of Calvinism as the dominant force in the national life, to which it rendered service of the highest value.

The first Reform movements in the Netherlands were independent of, and previous to, the inception of Calvinism. Before Luther's time there were signs which presaged the coming of a religious change, and when he came to the front his doctrines found wide acceptance. All this was to be absorbed in the more vigorous Calvinism. There were several causes for this. Lutheranism became the religion of the wealthier classes in the Netherlands and was at first only a protest within the Roman Church, while Calvinism was a popular movement and distinct in every way from Romanism. Then, too, the zeal and energy of the Huguenot preachers contributed a characteristic enthusiasm to the Reform that was highly effective. The superior organization of the Calvinistic body, also, was a most powerful instrument in the maintenance of Reformed teaching.

In the struggle with Spain all classes of Protestants united, but the leadership and moral force lay with the Calvinists. Their solidarity gave form to an otherwise scattered movement. As to the thinking that lay back of this series of events, a very suggestive quotation is made by Hausser from the Frisian records of this period: "Every one knows that the ruler is ordained of God to protect his subjects as the shepherd protects his flock. If, therefore, the ruler do not do his duty, if he oppress his subjects, destroy their ancient liberties and treat them like slaves, he is no longer to be considered as a ruler but as a tyrant. As such the country may justly and reasonably and honorably depose him and elect another in his place." In more than one thing this shows the influence of Calvin's teaching.

In the relation of Church and State in the Netherlands we find that the Genevan model was closely followed. Each maintained a separate government and code of laws; yet they were allied. The magistrates were to protect the churches in their work, and the preachers were by their teaching and moral influence to help the magistrate in the maintenance of law and order.

Not only in the crucial time of the Spanish war, but also in the succeeding time of peace, Calvinism did a great service in the building up of the Dutch Republic. This is easily lost sight of in the theological controversy between the Calvinists and Arminians, in which the latter are generally regarded as the progressive party. However this may be, from a political point of view we must draw different conclusions. Here Calvinists were the progressive, the Arminians the reactionary party. The greatest danger to the national life of the Dutch people came from within. The country was divided into petty states, each one of which was so assertive of its own rights as to endanger the general welfare. Nothing as yet, not even the long war with Spain, had welded them into a nation. In the Arminian dispute, the conflicting forces of local and central government came into collision in political, as well as in religious questions. The political parties joined in the controversy according to their predilection. There came thus to be a fourfold division in Netherlands society; the Calvinists favoring a centralized ecclesiastical authority vested in a national synod; the Remonstrants who contested the right of the synod to enforce its decrees on the minorities; the Orangeists who favored a centralized national government with the heir of the house of Orange at its head; and the advocates of extreme local government led by John of Barneveld, Grand Pensionary of Holland. The Calvinists threw in their lot with the Orange party and the victory was won for centralization. The struggle was renewed under Barneveld's successor, John de Witt, but he was not able to stem the tide. To the centralizing force of Calvinism is due largely the fact that the Netherlands ceased to be a mere collection of petty states and developed into a nation.

Calvinism in Scotland more than in the Netherlands was the creating of a nation. It might almost be said that before the Reformation there was no Scottish nation. It was only an association of fiefs and baronies, and the king himself was only chief baron, and possessed but little power. Out of this chaos of political uncertainties Calvinism wrought a nation, firm in its texture, enduring in its qualities.

The apostle of the Reformation in Scotland, John Knox, was a typical Calvinist and an example of how the Genevan Reformer inspired those who heard him or studied under him. On his return to Scotland he seemed to transfuse the Genevan Reformation into the life of the people. It was almost as if Calvin himself had come to repeat the work done on the Continent. Under the leadership of Knox, the Lords of the congregation were organized to protect the preaching of the gospel. But, as was true in the Netherlands, the real religious transformation was among the common people. A new spirit was infused into them. They became a unit in thought and aim and organization. The churches, the presbyteries, the synods, the general assembly as they were successively formed, built them up into a theocratic republic, stable, enduring.

A consistent book of discipline gave to the churches a constitution, elaborate and thorough, provided with method for administration, and method for exercising spiritual jurisdiction over its membership. Thus developed one of the strongest organizations ever known. Against it the Stuarts used all their power in vain, and indirectly at least they owe to it their downfall.

It is somewhat difficult to point out the direct political effect of Calvinism in Scotland, for the reason that its government became merged with that of England. But we may safely name the following: the nationalization of the Scottish people, the overthrow of feudalism, a more democratic quality in the parliament, thorough local administration of justice and the establishment of a fine system of free schools and universities through the country.

Stubbs, in his "Constitutional History of England," makes the statement that there are two great sources of English constitutional law, the ancient liberties and customs of the Angles and Saxons finding their completeness in local government, and the administrative system of the Norman conquerors superimposed upon and giving system to the local governments. The forces of English history so operated as to preserve both elements of constitution, and to fuse them so completely that the people were unconscious of the dual origin of their laws and liberties. At the time of the advent of Calvinism in England it found there a well established monarchy and a reformation, of a political kind at least, already accomplished. In a large measure the work which Calvinism did in Scotland and the Netherlands in a political way was here already accomplished.

Puritanism, the English form of Calvinism, made its appearance as a distinct type in the reign of Queen Elizabeth. The queen relied much upon the Puritans for support for they were intensely patriotic, but she distrusted them and repressed their earnest efforts for a complete reform. Calvinism as a whole never obtained the support of the government in England.

Besides this the endeavors of the Puritans were somewhat negatived by a division in the matter of church government. One party led by Thomas Cartwright held to a *jure divino* Presbyterianism. Another party, the Independents, advocated a separation of Church and State. So Calvinism never became in England the compact organization that it did in other countries. The contest between the Puritans and Charles I is illustrative of this fact. There were three parties in the struggle—the king, the Parliament, which represented Presbyterian uniformity, and the army, which was composed mainly of Independents. None of the parties represented ever completely attained its end. Presbyterianism never met with great success in England. It was the Calvinism of Cromwell and the army which gained the immediate victory, and which, later on, was to carry out a considerable part of its program.

Cromwell was a Calvinist in the political sense. He held to Calvin's idea of statecraft and tried to realize in England a political theocracy. That he failed is due not to his lack of genius, nor to inferiority in administration, but rather to the fact that his constituency was mainly of soldiers, and not of that class of men who were ordinarily chosen to form the parliament. He never could get a parliament that was in sympathy with his political ideals.

It is remarkable, however, that a large proportion of the political changes made by Cromwell have since become permanent. Among these we may mention the establishment of parliament as ultimate authority in place of the king, triennial sessions of parliament, the political union of Scotland and England, toleration of religious denominations, the abolition of illegal taxes, of the Star Chamber and the Court of High Commission.

The election by parliament of William of Orange as king of England was a demonstration of the change which Puritanism had wrought in English politics. A new conception of the relation of king and parliament is here expressed. William was not averse to this idea. Coming from a country imbued with Calvinistic thought he was at home in the new surroundings as the Stuarts could never have been, and he chose to uphold many of the reforms begun or suggested by the Puritans when in power.

That Calvin's theocratic idea had power and influence in America need hardly be said. The use of the Scriptures as a textbook in civil government by the early settlers in New England, their framing of constitutions on Bible principles and the effect of this example on the national constitution, are things familiar to all students of American history.

Griffis, in "Brave Little Holland," brings out the fact that the lessons presented by the history of the Dutch Republic did not pass unnoted by the framers of our constitution. They knew of the division that had weakened the national life of the Netherlands, arising out of the extreme devotion to local interests, and they saw to it that the American Colonies became a nation. In this way also Calvinism has had influence on American politics.

The country of France was the scene of great Protestant activity under the influence of the Genevan Reformation. We should expect that there also Calvinism would show its political power. But much has occurred to negative the legitimate effect of the Reformation in France. The terrible persecution and the extensive deportation of the Huguenots under Louis XIV diminished materially the effect of Calvinism, for those most devoted to its principles were the ones who suffered most.

Dr. Abraham Kuyper asserts that the Huguenots showed the same remarkable traits, with some natural exceptions, as the Independents in England. Especially was this true of their fundamental concept in politics. The sovereignty of God was

V. Applied Calvinism

the ruling thought, and out of this came the equality of men. Among the Huguenot towns and villages there was local government, popular suffrage and even trial by jury. They were nationally organized, also, through their synods, and formed a nation within a nation.

Baird also in his history of the Huguenots declares that though, since the times of Louis XIV, the French Protestants have been but a small minority, they have greatly influenced the political thought and life of the nation.

So it has come about that France, unlike the other Latin nations, is a republic. Calvin's ideas have permeated its social life in spite of persecution and prescription; but as the majorities which have carried these ideas into effect have been other than Protestant, they have become distorted and failed of complete accomplishment.

To a great extent, then, Calvin's political ideas have pervaded the Western nations, and even at this time, four hundred years after his birth, they are to be found expressed in institution and constitution, and incorporated into the body of our social consciousness.

VI. The Calvinistic Principle Of Authority

The period which follows the Reformation was one in which much stress was laid upon doctrine. The great change that had taken place was regarded as chiefly a doctrinal one, or a change that was due to a restatement of Christian truth. This emphasis upon doctrine led to a division of forces among the Protestant churches, for it accentuated the formal differences with the result of obscuring common interests. The result was an age of sectarian formalism. That underlying current of religious progress which really was the Reformation was checked, and in the surety that they had a perfect statement of divine revelation men ceased to ask for further improvements.

The Calvinistic principle which declared the Bible to be the inspired standard of thought and life, made of real authority by the action of the Holy Spirit on the heart, degenerated into the bare and unyielding assertion of verbal inspiration, until even the vowel points of the Hebrew text were looked upon as of divine giving.

Calvin's conception of an All-active God, intensely personal and in touch with every human being, became a definition expressed in infinite attributes, and philosophically a doctrine of fatalism.

His thought of the Christian life as an effort to be godlike was displaced by the idea of that life as the possession of a correct belief, and the effort of the preacher was too often a telling

VI. The Calvinistic Principle Of Authority

of the limits of orthodoxy, rather than the spiritual uplifting of his congregation. Protestantism seemed to have lost its constructive power.

Yet in the midst of all this formalism the spirit of the Reformation was still alive, though dormant. Principle still held good, though lacking expression. The spirit of Protestantism and the spirit of reconstruction were simply awaiting an opportunity to assert themselves. That opportunity has come. We live in the age of a new Protestantism and the principles thereof are strangely like those of the old, though the measures called for are of a different nature.

The intellectual battle of the Reformation centered about the question of authority. It was Bible against pope and Church. In the Protestantism of our own time the Bible has become again the center of discussion, but that which in the time of Calvin was radical has now become conservative; the battle is of the same nature, the battle-ground has been shifted. Again the progressive party asks for a new statement of religious truth and a new interpretation of the Bible itself; and it is busy with the endeavor to achieve this. "Let us know the truth," it has cried, "for the truth alone can bring God to us." Modern critical study has come in to make interesting once more the Bible of the Reformation fathers. But those who claimed to be, and were considered the doctrinal descendants of Calvin proved the most bitter opponents of the new movement. That this new movement was traceable back to the Reformation times and to Calvin himself was something altogether unrealized. But one has only to recall what a breaking away from old tradition, what a change in point of view, what an upsetting of old standards, the Reformation about Calvin was, to realize that the new critical attempt to understand the Bible is only a revival of Calvinism. Calvin dealt with the Bible critically. Certain books there were in the canon of the Scriptures that were called in question. These were examined as to their contents, their history investigated, and judgment rendered according to the evidence. But modern critics, treating for example the book of Esther in practically this same way, have been able to do so only amid a storm of protest, and have been laid under the charge of trying to destroy the Bible and undermine religious faith. It is not taken into consideration that the Bible is a collection of books, and that each book in the collection has to stand on its own merits, has always had to, and is in the Bible only because the ancient Church judged it worthy to be there; and this is something that Calvin realized and dealt with in careful critical investigation.

In our generation new material for critical work has come to hand; the scientific interpretation of the world, the principle of evolution, a new idea of inspiration, the discovery of new manuscripts relating to the history and texts of the Old and New Testaments, the deciphering of ancient inscriptions, discoveries in archæology external to the Bible, the study of comparative religion, all these call for treatment, interpretation and application for the purpose of throwing light on the nature of the Bible record, the manner of its construction, and the source of its moral and religious authority.

The critical effort to attain definite results from this material is not in spirit destructive. While it attempts to clear away some things considered outworn, its principal aim is reconstruction. Calvinism is historically the balancing of the elements of progress and conservatism. It happens to stand now for one, now for the other, or mayhap for both at the same time. It clears away old rubbish, it rears a new structure. Often it happens that the same man is first critic, then reconstructionist. So we are assured that a new conception of the Bible is coming to expression, which will afford just as true a basis of authority as before, and perchance a more reasonable standard of religious belief than that which we have received from our forefathers.

Now the very fact of the critical investigation of the Bible shows that authority in its ancient form is weakening. But man has a love for authority. It often is carried to such an extreme as to become an unnatural thirst for absolute infallibility. It matters not whether he is a philosopher scientist, historian, churchman or religionist, he makes infallibility his idol. He fashions it, not as the idol-makers of old with graving tool from wood or metal, but he takes the material of fact, or it may be of fancy, and with mind and pen fashions from it a standard of belief, a method of action, a metaphysical interpretation, and pronounces the work of his own mind infallible, a something absolute, a god, an idol in the world of thought and idea. Or it may be that the idol is found ready-made like the image of Diana at Ephesus, and he pronounces that to be perfect and infallible.

An ancient motto has come down to us, "*Semper, ubique et omnibus,*" always, everywhere, and among all, an infallible test of knowledge, the intellectual idol of the schoolmen. But it has been proved a false god, for time and again a single man has been right and all the world wrong; one man knows and all his fellows remain in ignorance. Science in one era is ignorance in the next, the civilization of one epoch becomes the barbarism of the next, while the heresy of past times may be the orthodoxy of the present.

The modern scientist makes his infallible by the method of induction and deduction. He looks over the whole field of known things until it seems to him that his collection of data warrants a universal induction; then he images an absolute principle and says to the world that this is a miniature of God and the universe. Then, too, the metaphysician with a like purpose before him carefully graves his intellectual idol, but perchance with much less reference to facts.

But the man untrained in the schools is often an idolator of this same class, for though he knows not the claim of the scien-

reached to the height of a divine self-revelation, and brought to culmination the age-long effort of the divine Will to express to the mind of man the reality of the spiritual as the final essence, and love as its true manifestation in God and man. That the content of religious consciousness varies greatly in different ages means not that authority and standard are lacking, but rather that they are becoming stronger and surer with each new religious experience realized and each new thought expressed; while as time goes on the essential things of morals and religion become more clearly evident, and the world races approach one another in sympathy and ideal.

But as one century succeeds another, even with the swift progress and growth of modern religious thought and consciousness, the effect is not to discount, but rather to throw into bold relief the Scriptures of the Hebrew race; for they were formed when the world was young, and in the beginnings of civilization, and in the absence of science and invention and real education, but yet satisfy the most cultured mind with their ideals of life and their vision of God, even though they may sometimes be cast in child language, or couched in figures of human existence. But more than all else is Jesus of Nazareth, anticipating in his moral life that type of manhood which the race may hope to attain only toward the close of its history, showing in his person that likeness to God which gives us our best understanding of the divine nature, and giving a personal, spiritual interpretation of God and man which alone grants to life a meaning beyond the merely sensual.

Hence the Bible is authoritative, is a standard not in a close, literal sense, not as a mere rule, but as giving an account of the best religious experience of the human race, the best thinking about God, the best life ever lived, and the best statement of those great moral and social principles upon which religious and civilized society must be built.

tist nor the prescription of the philosopher, yet he may exalt his own conscience into an absolute expression of right and wrong, or a faculty which will enable him to pass infallible judgment on all moral action in himself and others, and on the surety of his own conviction calls men to come and worship at his shrine. Or perchance the Church embodies for him the absolute, and its prescription for life and belief is infallible. He has only to obey its mandates and duty becomes plain, the pathway is clear and the gates of heaven stand open.

In the middle ages Roman pope and Church were the infallible for near all the Western world. The Bible was forgotten, science limited to a few of the more studious religious orders, and moral sense was dull. The Church was unchallenged. But with the emerging of a new era with its distrust of the papacy the old authority was undermined. Men sought a new infallible, and considered that they had found it in the writings of the Old and New Testament. The Bible became "an infallible rule of faith and practise."

But is Scriptural infallibility also an idol and have its worshipers been lead astray and taught to bow down to a mere intellectual image, which after all is not the real object of devotion?

"Infallibility" is not a Bible word. Such a thing is not claimed by the Scriptures for themselves. The word of self-commendation is simple and modest, "Holy men of old wrote as they were inspired." It is men who are inspired, not words or things. Calvin saw this clearly and plainly stated it, saying that the Scriptures had no true meaning except as the Spirit of God acted on mind and heart and enforced the truth therein contained.

But now if we still continue to regard the Bible as an "infallible rule of faith and practise," who shall be for us the authoritative interpreter? Protestant and Catholic, Lutheran and Calvinist, Episcopalian and Independent have varying interpretations of the same Bible, and within their ranks have sometimes almost irreconcilable differences. The infallible is still afar off. An infallible rule still needs an infallible application, and that the mind of man cannot furnish. The table of logarithms is useless in the hand of a child, and the child mind of man cannot infallibly use the eternal thought of the heavenly Father. The great Bible word is "Truth." This with "Love" forms the core of Jesus' thinking. The truth is what Jesus embodied, and love is the application of truth to human needs. Then it was not truth absolute that Jesus claimed to impersonate, but truth relative, relative to the world's moral and intellectual needs, relative to the progress of human history, relative to the development of social forces and individual experience, relative to the end for which the world of human kind was, and is. Absolute truth, infallible judgment are beyond the reach of the human intellect. To seek them is like chasing a will-o'-the-wisp.

Must Protestants then give up the objective principle of their faith? Do they lack a standard? Is authority dead, and must each man drift about on the uncertain sea of doubt, this one hither and that one thither? Surely not! Truth relative, standards changing progressively are far more real, and hence much more authoritative than an imagined inerrancy. The religious consciousness of the human race acted upon by the Spirit of God furnishes a standard of truth and morals relative to the needs of each age. Religious consciousness grows and develops, and thus progressing gains strength and clearness, and becomes an ever nearer approach to reality.

Herein is the significance of the Scriptures; they are the record of the religious consciousness and evolution of a race central in history and pivotal in spiritual human development. Prophets of the earlier, apostles of the later, period express in their thought and life the best and highest in God-consciousness and inspired activity that the race has ever attained to, while in the person of the Christ himself, this God-consciousness

VI. The Calvinistic Principle Of Authority

The history of the formation of the Bible canon illustrates how the race consciousness of religion attains to the authoritative. The books of the Bible are a collection, but further than this they are a selection. Not all, perhaps not half of the prophetic and historical writings of the Hebrews have been preserved for us. Frequent reference is made in the Old Testament to books which have passed out of existence, as the book of Jasher, the book of the prophet Nathan, while the apocrypha are only a part of a fairly extensive literature, allusions to which are made occasionally in the New Testament. Of the discarded books of Christian times we have a more definite knowledge. Not only their names but most of the books themselves are preserved and are accessible in English translation.

The final selection of the material for the scriptures of the Old Testament is supposed to have been made by Ezra with the help of the scholars composing the so-called Great Synagogue; the New Testament canon crystallized somewhere in the second century. In either case those books were selected which expressed the religious judgment and consciousness of the age, and which in the minds of men bore the mark of divine inspiration.

Our possession of discarded books, or apocrypha, especially of the New Testament, gives a norm of judgment as to what qualities in a book entitled it to a place among the sacred Scriptures, and as well what lack led to the discarding of others.

There would appear to be upon examination five forms of Scriptural material, the possession of one or more of which, in some acceptable literary form, and having evidences of inspiration, entitled a book to a place in the sacred canon. (1) History written to describe God's part in the religious development of the nation. (2) Revelation of the character of God. (3) Inspired standards of devotional conduct. (4) Inspired devotional writings. (5) Spiritual teaching in the form of parable or apocalypse.

The books which failed to make a favorable impression on the religious mind of the Hebrew and Christian will in general be found devoid of real religious helpfulness, and faulty in that they do not possess any of the above-named qualities. On the other hand millions of people turn to the recognized Scriptures today as they have for ages, and find help and comfort and inspiration.

And here the query naturally arises in the mind, If the writings of the Old and New Testaments are the record of the effect of God's Spirit on the life of man, and so are "Bible," why should not the effect of that same Spirit in subsequent eras produce material which might claim to be "Bible" also? Or, to change the form of the question, if as Calvin teaches, the Spirit of God is still acting on the mind and heart of man to the extent of enforcing Biblical truth, why should not that action now, as formerly, result in inspiration and the production of literary material of the same character and helpfulness as that in the Scriptures, and lead to a fuller knowledge of God and his ways and a better application of truth to life? Let us rather ask the question, Is not this just what has happened?

Our idea of God compels us to believe that he has ever ministered to the spiritual wants of man since his creation by some form of inspiration; it forbids us to think that human effort previous to the time of Abraham should have produced nothing in the way of literature that bore evidence of divine inspiration, and it is a contradiction of the words of Christ, "He shall guide you into all truth," to doubt that God is revealing himself more and more as Christian history progresses and that this revelation finds a continual expression in word and thought and life.

Thus is formed the larger Bible of the race, the fuller collection of divine knowledge, the ever-increasing history of religious experience, the whole literature of devotional expression, the growing spiritual consciousness of the whole world of men.

VI. The Calvinistic Principle Of Authority

Yet the ancient Bible is the Book of books and ever will be, just as Christ is King of kings, and Hebrew history is the middle point of religious history. Nothing can ever be written of such vast worth. The sacred literature of this central era of history stands by itself. We would insert no recent writings within the time-consecrated limits. There is a certain ideal culmination of revelation in the New Testament and in Christ which makes it impossible to conceive of a better man, of nobler moral teaching, or a finer concept of the character of God. Here are the fundamentals of our religion.

Nevertheless the thought and writing and religious experience of men of God since the time of the apostles are of high value as supplemental "Bible," and here and there in the great mass of literature shines out the story of the martyr, the song and prayer of the saint, the vision of the seer, the teaching of the prophet of God; and men finding in these things that for which their souls are hungering and thirsting thank God for an abiding inspiration.

A distinct feature of the life of Christian nations is the vast accumulation of scientific knowledge gained through discovery and invention. There is a seeking for truth in its every form, not only among the more highly educated people but also among the general reading public. This fact has an important religious bearing. The common knowledge of the greater discoveries made in the realm of science, especially in astronomy and geology, prepare the mind for a completer conception of the being of God. A mind whose knowledge included but a little world of a few hundred miles in extent, that conceived of the sun, moon and stars as but lights in the sky, that realized none of the laws of chemistry and biology and but little of the progress of human history, must perforce conceive of God in limited form as only a greater and better man, not an infinite, but only a larger finite being. But with us the telescope has revealed such vast and unthinkable distances in the universe that infinity seems a necessary thought in our concept of the God who is the origin of such a creation, while we at the same time easily ascribe infinite wisdom and power to the Being whose mind and will guide and control all the intricate movements of planet and sun and star. And on the other hand, chemistry with its analysis of the hidden relations of the different material elements suplements our idea of the infinite with the idea of the infinitesimal, that which is infinitely small, and reveals to us a control, not merely of the great things of the universe, but as well the very tiniest. Still further the record of theology preserved on the earth's surface, evidencing untold ages of world history, and telling us of the progress of life from its crude far-away beginnings up by continual development to those advanced forms which are now on the earth, offers a forceful suggestion of eternity, and gives a meaning to human life which it could not have as long as it were thought of as a sudden and immediate creation.

To this knowledge of God obtained through scientific discovery we must add that which we receive through the study of man's spiritual nature and spiritual experiences, and a much more important element in the larger Bible is the religious history which has been made since the time of the apostles. We are scarcely aware how much our thinking and character are influenced by religious biography and history, especially by that which is most recent and has come within the reach of our own vision. Preachers enforce the teachings they draw from the Scriptures with extensive illustration from Church history in all its different eras. The story of the conquest of the Roman empire by Christianity, the great struggle within the Church which we call the Reformation, the religious awakening under Wesley and Whitefield in England and America, the biography of great churchmen of all ages, the heroism of martyrs, the significant experience of common men, the stories of triumph in foreign missions, the development of different forms of devotional life, and above all the Christian life of those round about us in home and church, form a body of religious facts which has for us the force of "Bible," affording comfort, help and inspiration, becoming even revelation, for is not here registered the action of the Spirit of God on the world of people round about us?

We use different terms in describing the religious events and phenomena of recent times from what we do when referring to the facts of Bible history, and thereby we lose the significance of the wonderful things that are now happening in the world. We forget that "apostle" means "missionary," that "priest" is "only presbyter writ short," that "pastor" means "shepherd," that the Psalms are only a collection of hymns, that the Old Testament prophets were the great preachers of their times, and that their books consist largely of sermons; and we falsely conclude that there is only one "Holy Land" and only one period of inspiration. We have to make a distinct mental effort to realize that the deeds of modern missionaries are comparable with the acts of the apostles, and that Carey, Moffatt, Paton, Pattison, Chalmers and other modern apostles of the Christ, have a right to be associated with Peter, James and Paul as divinely appointed heralds of gospel truth and power to benighted peoples, and that their labors are no less wonderful, their sacrifice not less, God's spiritual presence with them no less in evidence, than when the word of Jesus was new in the world. Indeed, a review of the progress of missions since A.D. 1800 makes plausible the statement that the nineteenth century, next to the first, is the most important in the world's religious history, while today all over the earth as never before it is possible to trace the course of God's spiritual workings, and we have only to quicken our spiritual vision to look upon a future world where every land shall be a holy land, and every people a chosen people of God.

We have been wont to think of the Psalms as something in religious literature distinct from anything else ever produced. Our accustomed use of them, not so much in singing as in responsive reading in religious services, has contributed to this result. Nevertheless, we know that the Psalter is simply the hymn-book of the Hebrew religion, used as such to the present day, and that the Psalms were written to be sung in religious services and private worship. The English translation is not, however, so singable as the original Hebrew rendering, and while for a long time the Psalms held an exclusive place in the Protestant churches, slowly and gradually they have been supplanted as hymns, at first by metrical versions of themselves, and later by English hymns of recent composition and translations from other languages. We still read or occasionally chant the Psalms and are comforted and exalted by their truth and beauty, but the songs that we really sing are the product of modern psalmists, are the poesy of our hearts' devotion, in the language of our own time, and expressive of modern religious thought and life. Our finer hymns are the work of modern Davids and Miriams, of men and women who have lived near to God, and have had their natural poetic gifts enhanced thereby that they might give inspired expression to devotional truth in such a way as to comfort, guide and uplift the followers of Christ, as they render in word and song their personal praise and service. The psalm-book of the ancient Hebrews has expanded into a mass of song and praise, not gathered into any one collection, but found in many lands and rendered in diverse tongues, at times glorious and beautifully expressive, at others simple, even crude, but always heartfelt and sincere; the ways and means by which the human spirit in all its vicissitudes and experiences gives form to its aspirations, its ideals and its worshipfulness, just as, long years ago, the Jewish pilgrims on their way to festal service on Mount Zion found in the songs of ascent an expression of their

VI. The Calvinistic Principle Of Authority

own spiritual ambition and a way in which to worship Jehovah as they journeyed cheerfully along the uneven road.

The term "prophet" is another word for which we use a modern counterpart. Half unconsciously we give to the Hebrew teachers of God and preachers of righteousness such a deep and significant reverence as to obscure the greatness of the prophets of later times. We often speak as though there had been no prophets since John the Baptist, whom we think of as the "last of the prophets."

But we should grasp the truth that our latest period of history is fairly glorious with the names of prophets, not only among the ordained ministers of the gospel, but also among the laymen. Beginning with Savonarola, Wyclif and Huss, we have a long list of men who have been interpreters of God to men, who have pointed out the way of moral progress, who have championed the cause of religious reform, or given their strength and perhaps their lives also in the interests of freedom and brotherhood; and these have been and are our prophets. Because of the wealth of their prophecy the world of today fairly revels in truth, seems at times almost intoxicated with the deep drafts it inhales, while reform, progress and liberty follow the vision of truth with such surety and swiftness, as compared with former times, that our nerves are almost dulled by the rapid repetition of sensations, and we fail to appreciate the wonderful age in which we live, which, judged by actual progress, is in most ways the most wonderful of all history.

It is, then, a huge mistake to conclude that authority has come to an end. We have still all the authority of Bible truth, and though we have a different interpretation of that authority, we have one just as forceful as that which appealed so strongly to our forefathers. And to this we add the corroborative authority of later thought and experience and accomplishment, and conclude that in reality mankind is possessed of a surer religious sense and judgment than ever before.

But we might still be confused if we allowed the emphasis of authority to be placed upon creed, or the form of our intellectual belief. The true center of authority is not in the intellectual but in the moral realm; right living, not exact thinking, is the burden of Christ's message. From this point of view we can see how authority is gaining, not losing, under present conditions. Christ's moral and religious message is authoritative as never before. He has declared that God is our spiritual Father, and the new century counts by increasing millions those who thus looking upon God enforce the authority of this truth. He asserted the spiritual nature of man, and today this truth has come to greater power by the enlargement of experience, and because of the study of man's higher nature in a careful, scientific way and the discoveries consequent upon this study. Christ gave the world a picture of the righteous life, and made the offer of divine help to those who would follow in his steps, and each chronicle of history recounts the success of additional numbers of notable men who have realized the promise in a glorious way, while the rank and file of men possessing the same moral vigor give power to this word in the humbler circles of life.

Then, too, the growing sense of social obligation, the increase of practical brotherhood, and, most striking of all, the world-wide demand for freedom and equality of opportunity, and the recognition of the justice of this demand, make forcefully authoritative Christ's assertion of social duty as pictured in the parable of the Good Samaritan.

We reach then this conclusion: the religious consciousness of the race has come to have as its content a larger measure of truth, an increasing unity of expression, a common feeling of obligation under the terms of the fatherhood of God and the brotherhood of man, and an ever nearer approach to reality;

and there is created thereby a standard of authority, adequate to the conditions and demands of the present and perhaps for many future generations, or until a larger sense of truth and a diviner life shall afford a new and better basis of religious and moral judgment.

> "God is not dumb that he should speak no more;
> If thou hast wanderings in the wilderness
> And find'st not Sinai, 'tis thy soul is poor;
> There towers the Mountain of the Voice no less,
> Which whoso seeks shall find, but he who bends
> Intent on manna still and mortal ends,
> Sees it not, neither hears its thundered lore.
>
> "Slowly the Bible of the race is writ,
> And not on paper leaves, nor leaves of stone;
> Each age, each kindred, adds a verse to it,
> Texts of despair or hope, of joy or moan.
> While swings the sea, while mists the mountains shroud,
> While thunder's surges burst on cliff and cloud,
> Still at the prophets' feet the nations sit."

VII. The Elements Of Theocracy

The theocratic government of Geneva has been the object of a good deal of criticism. It is looked upon as autocratic, oppressive, one-sided, and for all but that time and place, impractical, an attempt to realize the impossible. But criticism often confuses the essential and the incidental elements of the Genevan theocracy, failing to note that the more objectionable things in the governmental policy of the city did not necessarily appertain to a government of this character, but are just as likely to appear under any form of administration.

In general, we understand theocracy to mean a form of government wherein the attempt is made to have a divine direction given to the affairs of State; God is the real sovereign, the rulers and prophets are his agents and interpreters; the citizens of the nation are first of all citizens of the divine kingdom; laws obeyed or broken imply acts in obedience or defiance of God's will, and crime is in its essence a sin against God.

The fact that these principles were given application in Geneva does not of itself furnish ground for hostile criticism. The emphasis of the critic rests elsewhere. Certain restrictions on liberty of belief, some rather tyrannical sumptuary regulations, unduly harsh laws and rigid execution of them, are largely responsible for what odium attaches to the common idea of theocracy. Furthermore, a conclusion was drawn from the idea of crime as a sin against God that was unwarrantable. It was declared not only that a crime was a sin against God, but also

VII. The Elements Of Theocracy

that a sin against God was a crime and punishable as such by the magistrate. But this was going beyond the divine commission, even as stated by the theocrat himself, that the magistrate is ordained of God for the administration of public affairs, for the maintenance of peace and order and the support of public worship; for there is a part in the being of each individual which is outside of the reach of government, and for which he is not responsible to his fellow men, but only to God. It is really a contravention of theocracy when the State attempts to take cognizance of the inner life of the man. It steps in between the subject and his real sovereign. The execution of law reaches only the outward act of theft and murder, and has no administrative concern with the state of mind and heart which leads to such acts. It is true that the State is deeply concerned in the moral character of its citizens, and may change environment and alter conditions to favor the best moral development, but it cannot enforce the moral law on the inner man. The attempt to make people good by legislation is foredoomed to failure.

The Genevan theocracy had the appearance of being autocratic, and unconsciously our conception of what constitutes a theocracy is tinged with this idea, and we feel as though a government which tried to repeat the Genevan experiment could not be a government by the people and for the people. But it is for us yet to discover that theocracy may come to its noblest manifestation under democracy, and be the more truly what its name implies because not one, or a few, but the many constitute the agency by which the divine will for the nation may come to practical expression.

It is scarcely possible to come to any idea of government without giving it a theological basis of some sort. Morals, order, justice, equality, association are as characteristic of religion as of the State, and in either case they are traced back to their origin in the will of God. And there are, after all, but a few alternatives for a theological foundation of government. Three typical forms of government present themselves: (1) Theocracy, based on the idea of a personal God, the Jehovah of nations, who is the real sovereign; (2) Positivism, allied to agnosticism, which seeks within man himself all the principles necessary for law and government and morals; (3) Pantheism, based on the idea of an impersonal deity who reaches expression in all forms of life, and the highest expression in the most intellectual being.

Christian thought finds but one of these acceptable. It demands a theocracy in some form whether it prefers this name or some other. Even in the first era of the Church, the apostles taught their followers to obey the magistrates as representing a divine order and authority in society, and now that Christianity has come to be the dominant religion of many nations, it is to be expected that its doctrine of God should find expression in law and government.

Calvin was a theocrat. In extended and forceful argument he taught away the distinction which medieval society had made between the sacred and the secular; Church and State were to him equally manifestations of the divine will—God's will for the individual man lost in sin, and God's will for the man in the social and political relations of life. At Calvin's suggestion civil government and church government had a joint establishment in Geneva for the purpose of creating a truly Christian society. In general it was a thoroughgoing success. The moral and religious condition of the city was vastly improved, the intellectual standard of the people was raised, government was made efficacious, industry became prosperous, while the city's influence, upon the rest of Switzerland and upon Europe, remarkably exceeded its relative political importance and wealth. Some of the methods employed, even some of the purposes stated were unwarranted, to say the least, but in the main the results at-

VII. The Elements Of Theocracy

tained were a justification of the larger purpose of the Genevan theocracy.

When Calvin first attempted to put into operation his theocratic ideas in the government of Geneva, he so roused the hostility of the more licentious portion of the populace that he was forced into exile, and the attempt seemed for a while a complete failure. But the anarchy and license, which followed the removal of his strong influence from the city, brought the better classes of the people to the conclusion that even a strict theocracy was preferable to disorder, and when Calvin returned upon their invitation, it was to become and remain for the rest of his days the dominant force in the city's life. He was not able to bring about all the changes that he desired, but in the main his plans and policies were carried out in both Church and State, to such an extent that he was the virtual ruler of the city though holding no civil office.

There is no dispute, then, as to the statement that the government of Geneva under Calvin was a theocracy, in so far as human wisdom and effort could make it so. His teaching was that Christ was supreme both over the Church and over the State—his will and teaching were to be followed in the one as in the other.

It is fortunate for later developments that the theocratic plan was applied in so significant a case, in a government whose formal structure was democratic. Calvin himself did not have any special predilection for any one form of government as over against another, either in civil or religious affairs, and his personal feeling was somewhat aristocratic. Nevertheless Calvin's intellectual conceptions and theological teachings were thoroughly democratic both in theory and application, and the field of the Genevan Republic was soil singularly fitted for the growth of his planting.

The foundation thought of the Calvinistic democracy is the so-called doctrine of the priesthood of all believers; whether then, a man regard himself as a church member or a citizen he takes his privilege and his duty direct from God. This is the essence of the theory; in application it must have organized form. With Calvin it took the shape of two autonomies, one for civil and one for religious life. The citizens of one were the members of the other, but the two activities were kept distinct, at the same time being very closely allied, and similar in gradation and structure. In either case the foundation of government was the people. The republic had two councils with legislative powers, and four syndics as administrators of public affairs. The Church had as a legislative body a consistory made up of both lay and clerical members, and its policies were carried out by the Venerable Company, a body made up of the pastors of the city. With such a form of organization the Genevese set out under Calvin's influence and guidance to establish a purely Christian society.

In describing the different steps in the formation of this theocracy it may be best to pass by Calvin's first efforts, which were followed by his banishment, and take up the progress of things subsequent to his recall in 1541.

The immediate cause of Calvin's exile had been his insistence upon a strict discipline in the management of Church affairs, which included an oath on the part of the citizens not only to abide by the discipline, but also to accept the confession of faith. Before Calvin accepted the invitation to return, he stipulated that this discipline and confession should be a part of the fundamental law of the republic; every citizen was to subscribe thereto; and as the material for these documents was derived from the Bible, this was equivalent to an oath of obedience to the divine law as there expressed.

Following closely in logical order after the book of discipline came the catechism, the purpose of which was to educate

VII. The Elements Of Theocracy

the people in the knowledge of Christian doctrine; and as a sequent development of this there followed the establishment of a system of elementary schools, the main intention of which was to make it possible for every citizen to read the Bible for himself and learn therefrom directly the lessons of truth and life, and by so doing to become worthy members of the theocracy. There was established also an academy, a higher institution of learning, which was intended as a training-school for teachers and preachers and religious scholars; the republic was by this means to be supplied with educated and worthy leaders and pastors.

Church and school having been provided for, it remained to revise the civil law according to a Biblical plan. A high standard of citizenship was set up and laws were enacted for the purpose of bringing every citizen up to this standard. These laws were strict to burdensomeness. Attendance at religious services was obligatory, education was compulsory, gambling, drunkenness, loafing in taverns, profanity, extravagance, immodesty in dress, irreligious songs, immoral novels and other books, heresy, worship of images and blasphemy were forbidden in the new code of laws and transgressions of them were severely punished. It might almost go without saying that these laws were not finally established until a battle had been fought, but that battle over and the libertine party vanquished, the theocracy proceeded triumphant on its way and made of Geneva the capital of the Reformed Church.

One more thing came within the reach of the theocratic purpose. The government initiated a policy of industrialism which was called for by the exigencies of the situation. Refugees came from many lands to the famous city and they had to be provided for. Work was given them. Old industries were expanded, new industries introduced, so that Geneva became as remarkable for its thrift as its religion. But without these peculiar conditions it would have been thoroughly in accord with the theocratic principle to care for the industrial as well as the religious needs of the people; for the whole range of human activities and interests is through the working out of this principle brought under control for beneficent ends.

But what is the historic import of this achievement of Calvin's? Has it a fruitage in modern conditions at all comparable with that of his theological work?

To answer this query we shall need first of all to remove from the Genevan theocracy those elements that are purely local or non-essential. We may drop, then, the peculiar form of government which was partly of native origin and partly the work of Calvin. We may take away also the unnecessary strictness of law and the harshness of its enforcement. Again we may deny that a sin against God is necessarily a crime to be dealt with by the magistrate, and again we may allow a freedom of behavior, of worship and of faith.

When we have done this, our conception of theocracy will be: (1) that the real ruler of the nation is the eternal personal God; (2) that the laws of nations should be based upon and be expressions of the moral order divinely established; (3) that the rulers are such for the purpose of maintaining this order with equivalent justice for all; (4) that it is the work of organized society, Church and State, to provide for the moral and material improvement of the people within their jurisdiction; and in a truly Christian society to apply the principle of brotherhood to every department of life.

Theocracy possessing these salient features along with local peculiarities is easily recognized in the Dutch Republic, in England under the protectorate of Cromwell and in New England in its early history. But it is not understood how thoroughly theocratic principles have pervaded law and life in the great American republic of today, nor is it understood that it is the adoption of these principles that differentiates the United States

VII. The Elements Of Theocracy

from other nations having similar constitutions and purporting to be sister republics. But the truth is that no other people in history, not even excepting the Jewish nation, were ever so theocratic as the American people of the present time, or have tried to realize with such sincerity and devotion ideas of life derived from Scriptural teaching. The theocratic idea never had so great opportunity nor so vast expression. No such mass of people were ever so responsive to divine leadership or tried so unitedly to carry out the divine will. It is an unpardonable error to think of the American people, as so many do, as entirely carried away by the commercial spirit. It is easy to be misled by appearances, for the industrial life of America is so gigantic and requires such a huge army of workers, and involves so much time and thought and effort spent on purely material aims, that there seems neither room nor time for anything else. But it is only seeming. Americans are above all idealists. In the midst even of their commercial pursuits, they are thinking of and working for ideal conditions under which to conduct industry and apportion the results of labor. They have a noble ideal of national life and for the individual man a type no less noble. Freedom and spontaneity they seek in their religious life. The New England home with its exaltation of womanhood has become the nation's ideal, and a new love and appreciation of childhood is taking possession of the land. The educational scheme includes all children and in most parts of the country instruction is free until the completion of the high school course. There is also an eager longing for art that is typically American, for music that shall beat in a new-world rhythm and for a literature that shall voice the ideal, as well as the real, in American life.

Theocracy has its real opportunity in a republic. It is a false notion that couples it with aristocracy, and in America where approximately a third of the population are members of Christian churches, and nearly as many more are under Christian instruction, and millions of others are but less closely connected with church life and work, and all of these in conscious unity look to God as their heavenly Father to whom first obedience is due, the force of moral influence thus generated is simply incalculable, it is a thing such as never was before and it perforce makes the nation theocratic whether it will or no.

If we turn to American law and the Constitution we shall be impressed with the theocratic character of their make-up. It is stated on good authority that the Constitution of the United States was modeled on the constitution at that time in force in the state of Connecticut, which in turn was founded on the Scriptures. Whether this be true or not, the Constitution certainly carries out the leading social thought of the gospel. The purposes expressed in the preamble and provided for in the text are unity, justice, peace, defense, common welfare, liberty. The Bible is not mentioned nor the name of God used in any part of the document, but it is nevertheless true that the Christian principles of government never were so fairly stated in any national constitution. There is no provision for an established church, but for all that no churches ever had so firm a constitutional basis as the American. No document of its kind, perhaps, has so little to say about religion, none so much to do with real religious principles. The political equality demanded, the brotherhood principle of unity, the personal liberty assured, the purpose of promoting the general welfare, are practical applications of Christian teaching to the theory and practise of government. The chief magistrate as he enters upon his office takes solemn oath that he will "preserve, protect and defend" the Constitution, and it is prescribed in that Constitution that he is to "take care that the laws be faithfully executed." And what the President is required to do is expected of other magistrates in their own special sphere of activity; they pledge themselves

VII. The Elements Of Theocracy

as servants of the people to carry out the purposes of the law and Constitution.

A review of the laws which presidents and governors are required to see executed, reveals most clearly the theocratic nature of the American commonwealth, and the resemblance of American laws in purpose and form to those of sixteenth-century Geneva is remarkably striking, and while it is true that they are not so drastic, and omit some of the subjects of Genevan legislation, it is to be noted that in many ways they reach out beyond the limits of effort in the older republic; for new conditions have arisen, in the more complex life of today, which call for the application of law upon things which in simpler times could be trusted to care for themselves.

This finds an apt illustration in the laws and provisions which concern child life. The laws providing for free and compulsory education have as their objective a nation composed of educated citizens. Conditions do not favor extensive religious teaching in the public schools, but still a certain moral discipline is insisted on that in most cases is of remedial force. In addition to this is the more important fact that a very large proportion of the teaching force is composed of Christians, the influence of whose example and behavior goes far to make up for a formal teaching of religion. And we may add to this the custom which prevails in many states of reading from the Scriptures at opening exercises. And the conviction is growing stronger with each year that passes that a mental training is useless, is oftentimes even dangerous, unless it be accompanied by a moral education. The theocratic purpose of the public schools of America finds expression in a roundabout way, but it is theocratic after all—the schools exist for the purpose of providing the nation with educated Christian citizens.

But modern legislation goes beyond the mere educational care of the children; it provides homes for those that are orphans, asylums for those that are blind, deaf and dumb, and special institutions for the defective. It seeks also to protect the child from parental abuse, and is beginning to insist with increasing strictness that the child shall not be exploited as an industrial factor by either parent or employer. The cities are assuming the hygienic care of the children in their schools, are providing industrial training for both sexes and furnishing playgrounds, gymnasiums, baths and reading-rooms. By ever-increasing effort the American people seek to establish the best conditions possible for child life. It is heresy now to leave uncared for the progress of a child's life; it is more than that, it is crime.

The Church was formerly the agency which cared for the poor and the dependent. A theocratic spirit in the State has taken this office in large degree away from the Church and thereby creates a benevolent institution, not always showing the same sentiment and sympathy as the other body, but perchance many times distributing with a more even justice and greater wisdom. A vast sum is spent every year by the different states for benevolent purposes, and the express purpose of laws regarding this subject is, that every dependent person, of whatever age or sex, shall have some place of abode, plentiful though plain food and the simpler comforts of life. The dependent insane are cared for in public institutions, free hospitals are becoming common, while movements are on foot for the establishing of sanitoriums for tuberculous patients who are unable to provide needed treatment for themselves. In the great cities benevolences assume enormous proportions and extend even to the hygienic care of people and places and the inspection of milk and meat and other food products. And the end is not yet.

Quite recently public attention has been called to a new movement in the administration of criminal justice. The purpose of this project is not so much punishment for so much crime, but the improvement and reform of the drunkard and

VII. The Elements Of Theocracy

the criminal of milder type. It is a system of probation. The court takes a parental care of such delinquents as come before it, and they are allowed freedom during good behavior and are individually watched over by some officer appointed for that purpose by the court. Of like character and purpose is the juvenile court of some American cities wherein the judge acts *in loco parentis* for young offenders. Through these institutions the State takes on the character of a remedial organization, combining moral influence with authority. This whole policy of caring for those who cannot or who will not take care of themselves, is thoroughly theocratic in its nature and is characteristic of Christian countries and most of all the United States.

A like tendency is to be seen in efforts dealing with the industrial problem. The American people have never taken kindly to the doctrine of *laissez faire*. At one time a large party sincerely advocated an absolute freedom of trade. But the purely doctrinaire position on this subject has been practically abandoned by publicists, and in its place has come a sense, national and unsectional, which looks for an intelligent care of industrial interests of all kinds on the part both of national and state governments. Instead of violent and extended arguments about the tariff, public speakers are busy with a new program, a gospel of fair play and just wages for the worker, a gospel of responsibility for the owners of wealth, and a gospel which preaches the common interest of the people at large in the face of both contesting parties. Slowly and surely this gospel is being written into law and statute. So we have laws limiting the hours of labor, requiring weekly payment of wages; employers' liability laws, enforcement of safety appliances on railroads and many other provisions of like import. Efforts are being made to give the government at least a partial control of wealth through inheritance or income taxes, but more especially through laws relating to interstate commerce, insisting upon equitable transportation rates and upon the quality of food products to be offered for sale outside of the producing state, and through laws forbidding unjust combinations in restraint of trade. The reform along this line seems to have but begun. In an advisory way also the national government attempts the leadership and instruction of the people by departments devoted to agriculture, manufactures and labor. All this has been termed in a detractive way "paternalism"; but instead of being a nickname, this word, taken in its nobler meaning, or a word of equivalent sense, will be used to describe the theocratic attitude of modern government toward the industrial interests of the people.

More strikingly, but not more really, is this principle shown in laws which have as their purpose the moral defense or improvement of the people. We have long had laws enforcing with considerable strictness the cessation of common labor on the Sabbath, laws forbidding gambling, immoral books, pictures and plays, prostitution, public obscenity and profanity. But undoubtedly the greatest effort and greatest success of this kind has been the movement to stifle the liquor traffic. A century of temperance agitation is coming to a close in this nation. It finds whole states given to the policy of prohibition; large sections in other states pursuing the same policy, while a growing sentiment and a wiser use of law bid fair to win for this cause a complete victory ere long. And when this work shall be done it is not likely that the American people will be satisfied to endure other evils of a related nature, but will through agitation and law enactment effect a still better moral environment for themselves and their children.

But America is not alone in possessing this theocratic force. We find it also in England and her colonies; it is represented by parties at least in Germany, Holland, Belgium and France; and even Spain and Italy, wonderstruck at American progress, are coming into sympathy with the methods by which this progress is being achieved. A social miracle has come to pass in Turkey, and in the Far East Japan is reflecting the influence of American thought; while even China seeks to care for the moral welfare of its many millions by the prohibition of the opium habit. In every nation on the earth the gospel of Christ and the eternal Father is being preached and lived. A new unity is coming to the world in thought and feeling, in law and government, in type of living. The foundation is being laid for a world republic pervaded by Christian ideas and guided by Christian purposes. Theocracy has not ended. It has just begun.

VIII. The Dynamics Of Protestantism

There is considerable familiarity in common thinking with the statics of the Reformation,—creed, tradition, convention, statistics, polity, theology and historic facts. There is not such familiarity with the dynamics of the Reformation,—those forces and principles which, coming to expression in the sixteenth century, really produced that great movement.

It is possible to take a photograph of a river that is wonderfully real, or for the artist to depict a landscape with line and color so true that the eye is almost deceived. But in either case the likeness never changes, the river flows not away, the grass waves not in the breeze, changes of season never come; nothing ever grows or moves in a picture. There is a reality and a beauty which the artist can never put upon canvas, the great truth of change and growth and the poetry of motion. His art is only a window, through which we look out upon the world of men and things, and see the ceaseless movement that is taking place, and infer the tremendous forces that are at work everywhere in the universe.

It might be possible to write a history of the Reformation which would have the true accuracy of the photograph, or a series of photographs, or have the visional quality seen in the masterpieces of the painter's art, that yet should not reveal to the eye of the mind those elementary forces that were the cause of all this history, and only suggest to the imagination that ceaseless and irresistible current of modern thought and life which has brought the Western world to its present state of progress and development.

There is an interpretation of Protestantism which declares that this great movement has reached its culmination and accomplished its mission; that its theology, ethics and philosphy are overpast, and we must look to some new social and moral force by which to move the world along. But this is the static interpretation of the Reformation which describes not the forces in the army of progress, but only its halting-places, its battle-grounds, its fortifications, its victories and defeats.

But the question which interests us is whether or not the dynamics of the Reformation are still in operation in Christian society, and whether or not they are highly usable forces in the exigencies of modern life.

The Reformation came to England and America chiefly in the form of Calvinism. We are aware, however, that Calvinism is not the entire Reformation, but only a phase in its development. We can explain Calvinism only as we look a generation further back to the work and teachings of Luther and Zwingli. But we may not even stop there. If Calvinism had its impetus from Lutheranism, it is also to be said that Lutheranism gained its initial force from what had gone before. The difference between Luther and Calvin on the one hand, and Wyclif and Huss and Jerome of Prague on the other, is not enough to explain why the Reformation came in the sixteenth and not in the fourteenth century. The real difference was not in the men or in their thinking; it was in the social and religious life of those two centuries. When the earlier Reformers spoke they voiced chiefly their own thoughts. When Luther and Calvin spoke they voiced the thought and feeling of their own nations and time. A remarkable change had in the meantime come over Europe. Intellectual and moral forces had been created and set in motion, and the success of the later Reformers was largely due to the fact that they gave direction to these new forces, expressed them in terms of religious thought, and blessed them with lives singularly devoted and full of good works.

The term "Protestantism" is for several reasons inadequate to describe the thing it represents. It stands for negation, or opposition to some established ways or forms; the word has in itself nothing of a constructive nature and is suggestive of that which is only temporary. By association and interpretation it has come to mean much more than its derivation implies, but it needs continual elucidation and description.

As already suggested, Protestantism is twofold in its make-up. It is an organized protest against that which is false and unreal in traditional teaching, custom and law, and is forceful even to iconoclasm. But its spirit is not destructive. It abolishes, only that it may replace with something better. It destroys, only that it may rebuild on larger lines, and it is this characteristic that is the essential one in Protestantism. In other words Protestantism is a great impulse toward progress, a craving for better things, and an effort to bring about changes in the life and thought of the world that are in accord with the teaching of Christ. It is not content with things already done, no matter how great or important. It is satisfied only in action. Protestantism at rest is Protestantism dead. An ancient motto expresses the spirit of this great movement in a beautiful way:

"Do ye nexte thynge."

We should make a great mistake also if we tried to interpret Protestantism as a movement altogether in the realm of the Church. The religious Reformation in Europe served as the foremost expression of that great impulse which characterized the sixteenth century, but not the exclusive one. A great intellectual awakening had come in between the earlier and the later Reformers. The scholastic philosophy was no longer satisfacto-

VIII. The Dynamics Of Protestantism

ry; there was a longing for expression in the sympathy felt for the mysticism of Tauler, for the Biblical teaching of Colet, More and Erasmus. There was also a growing sense of national life, which was to lead ere long to a great social and political change in Europe. In fact every interest in life responded to the new impulse, and when the Church Reformers took their stand in the forefront of the progressive party, it meant that the religious thought of Protestantism should leave its stamp upon every product of the new culture.

It must be remembered, also, that the movement described under the name "Protestantism" was not confined in its efforts and results to the Reformed Church. It was first a movement within the Roman Church. As an intellectual movement it began in Italy, following the advent of Greek scholars after the fall of Constantinople. It took its first form in the Italian universities, and was patronized by the popes themselves. Pope Leo X, who was on the throne when Luther began his reform work, was enthusiastic in his devotion to Greek learning, and established a college at Rome especially for the study of the Greek language and literature. Then, too, the first steps in reform were taken by men who looked for a moderate reform within the Roman Church, without schism. Even Luther at first so thought and planned, and it was only as he was driven out of the old communion that it occurred to him to form a new organization. Subsequently when the Church had split over the question of limited or extensive reform, the passion for moral and spiritual improvement was not confined to the more radical section. There was a reform within the Roman Church as evidenced among other things by the formation of the Society of Jesus, with its purpose of perfect devotion to Christ and conquest of the world for him. And though the results are not so apparent as in the Reformed bodies, owing to the fact that little outward change was made, they were after all just as real within their more limited range.

With this view of the larger Protestantism before us, we shall be able more clearly to describe the forces which might be called its dynamic principles.

The first great dynamic of Protestantism is the assertion of personality. Some kind of philosophy underlies every great thought-movement. Some noble conception is back of every reform. Yet it would be inaccurate to say that there is a metaphysic of Protestantism in any definite systematic form. Many systems of philosophy might be constructed within the field of Protestant ideas, according as one principle or another were assumed as the starting-point. But from the standpoint of the practical, and with the religious purpose in view, we easily come to the great premise upon which Protestant thinking is based.

The theology of Protestantism is founded on a pure theism. Anything but a personal God is abhorrent not only to its thought, but also to its feeling; the whole heart and soul of it is Jehovah, who enters into the life of all men as Creator, Spiritual Father, Saviour and Judge, the dominant personality of the universe. The exact form in which Calvin presented this thought we are not obliged to follow. Some other term than "decree" will describe for us the powerful, personal way in which God enters into our lives and makes his will felt in the progress of history. But the real content of our thought is the same as that of Calvin's; we only clothe it with different language, and attempt its definition in the light of that added knowledge which modern science and research has brought to us.

In accordance with this conception of God there follows logically a philosophy of idealism in some form, not necessarily absolute, or altogether free from a temporary dualism, but nevertheless a practical philosophy within the reach of the common mind; it is idealism in the sense that it presents spirit as the first and ultimate being and substance in the universe; what we term matter is only a manifestation of spiritual thought and power. We are taught to look back of matter for reality and beyond it for life. We thus find our place in the world. We, too, are ultimately spirit, not matter, and share, if we will, in the divine qualities of spirit, holiness and eternity.

The stricter Protestantism of the Reformed Church insists most strenuously upon the proposition that each man is his own priest, and can come into personal spiritual relations with the Father Spirit without the intermediation of priest or pope. This has given origin to a strong doctrine of individualism which is taught in books, promulgated in constitutions and expressed in life. It is one of the great forceful things of modern life, so assertive, in fact, that we are now busy restating the principle in terms of social obligation. The practical value of this conception is the sense that it gives each man a possession and place in God's world. From this individualistic point of view, society as an organization is seen to be only a means to an end, not an end in itself. Society exists as a protection and environment for individuals, not "the individual," nor some individuals, but all the individuals that enter into it. Society is the household of men. It is their united will, their collective purpose, their family dwelling-place, their commonwealth; and the condition of any nation is to be judged, not by the totality of its wealth and power and its scholarly productions, but by the average wealth, the intellectual powers, the moral character of all the individuals who are its citizens. For society is only individuals, justly and helpfully brought into relation to one another through birth, association and law.

Individualism is often treated as though it came in conflict with social interests. This appears to be true oftentimes. But a careful investigation will reveal in such cases a one-sided individualism, an individualism, that is, of some at the expense of others, as perchance of the rich and strong as over against the poor and weak. But this is not the true practise of individualism, for individual rights mean common rights, universal rights, and as far as this subject goes, law and freedom are interchangeable terms. In the real practise of this principle, where each man is treated with justice and respect for his personality, it will be assured that not only shall he have equal rights before the law, but also in life he shall have equivalent opportunity with all other men.

The intense conviction of personality, both human and divine, which is so characteristic of Protestantism leads to a principle of ethics. We need not stop to classify this principle philosophically. We seek only the practical and actual application of a great idea. Protestantism places its ethical emphasis on the will of God. As God is the great personality, the ruler over all finite personalities and the one to whom responsibility is due, it follows easily that men to fulfil moral ends must do and be what God wills for them; for the very nature of morals involves, after a provision for self-development and position, a relation with others, and because God is greater than all others, the main moral relationship must be with him. The moral man is then the one who seeks to carry out God's will. We need not stop to consider whether the *summum bonum* is usefulness, happiness or goodness; whatever it be, the fulfilment of divine law or the effort to that fulfilment will lead to the highest good. The ethical principle of Protestantism is personal, not formal.

The second dynamic of Protestantism is the assertion of the supremacy of reason. Protestantism was, and is, an appeal to reason as over against tradition and authority. The Reformers generally were ever ready to argue their positions and were capable of doing so. It is true that they used the Bible as an authority in place of the Church. But they reasoned themselves to this position also. Something must represent God and the truth. In the Bible they found that something; it was a revelation of God to them; they therefore concluded that herein was true authority, and they set up that authority as above Church and prelate because it seemed reasonable to do so.

It has been charged against Protestantism that it is essentially rationalistic in its tendency. Whether this be true or not depends altogether on the definition of rationalism. If it is taken in the metaphysical sense whereby a leading idea is chosen as a main assumption, and the universe is reconstructed according to this idea without regard to what has taken place, or been recognized as authority in the past, then Protestantism is certainly not rationalistic. Protestantism has a great reverence for the past of men and ideas, a reverence, however, not slavish, nor blind. It finds in former history the working of God's spirit, while it expects that working to be continued in the future.

In two things Protestantism may be said to be rationalistic in the simpler and truer meaning of the term. In the first place it attempts to pass judgment by careful reasoning on the worth of things as it finds them. This was the first great task of the Reformation. One by one the ideas, doctrines and methods in vogue in Church and State were called up before the bar of reason and pronounced good or bad, as they were adjudged to be in accord or not with the principles of righteousness and truth as expressed in the Bible, the reasonably accepted standard. There were no exceptions made intentionally. Everything was challenged, and in so far as they were able and had understanding, they let no false word or custom pass on into future use.

In the second place the spirit of reason showed itself in a progressive way. The Reformation was not merely a court of justice, it was also a legislature and an executive. The laws of religion, morals, politics and social life were restated, and new laws were enacted and promulgated by a method of constructive reasoning based on the same principles of truth and righteousness by which they had estimated the worth of things past.

With a sublime faith these men of reason set out to do the things which the legislative mind had formulated as ideal, and thereby initiated the second great stage of the Reformation, the period of reconstruction, in which we find laid the foundation of our modern civilization.

These two applications of reason have been continuously characteristic of Protestantism. It is quite likely to happen in this era that the position of challenge is taken toward the new idea, so that it seems at times as if Protestantism shrunk from the legitimate results of its own methods of reasoning. The Copernican astronomy, the teachings of Galileo, the philosophy of evolution, the uniformity of natural law, the critical study of the Bible and other things not so worthy, have partly taken the place of ancient tradition as the objects of challenge and criticism. It is evident, nevertheless, that Protestantism has not lost its rational principle, for one by one as these new subjects have come up for adjudication they have found acceptance or rejection, altogether or in part, as evidence is weighed and sifted, as truth comes more and more to light, and judgment is passed as careful reason dictates. And whenever a great truth comes thus to favor, legislative Protestantism reformulates its statement, promulgates it, and makes it a part of a great world program of progress and enlightenment. An ever-repeated process of challenge, of justification or condemnation, of careful reconstruction, ensures to the modern world that same vitality and power of development which began in Europe with the Renaissance.

The third dynamic of Protestantism is the assertion of freedom. This does not appear so plainly on the surface of things as do some other of the great facts of the Reformation. When thinking upon this subject our attention fixes itself upon certain great heroes whose dominant personalities impressed themselves very forcibly on the thinking and life of the time. These men gathered about them a large following of those who accepted their ideas *in toto* and so formed schools of thought and religion that became international in character. Their bulk and influence overshadowed other men and their efforts, and their power proved a temptation toward uncharity which they were not able to resist. These men claimed freedom to think for themselves, this was the important thing. That they failed to extend freedom to men who believed otherwise detracts from their glory, but not from the meaning of their acts. When Luther nailed his theses upon the door of the Castle church at Wittenberg, the thing was done and could not be undone. Henceforth men were to think, not as their superiors told them to think, but as their own experience and reason led them to think. Luther did not show charity to Anabaptists and Zwinglians because he could not reconcile their tenets with his understanding of the Bible. But they had only repeated his cry. These men also claimed liberty to think as they would, and with them were many others, Calvinists, Covenanters, Puritans, Independents, Freethinkers, men of the utmost variety of thought and belief made a common claim,—liberty of thought, of speech and of worship.

Because of this common demand for freedom, even in the face of uncharity and hatred, Protestantism is to be characterized as a movement for freedom of thought; and it required only the passage of a sufficient amount of time and the suppression of an extreme class distrust, to make the thing clear in men's minds and a realized thing in their life. In the Protestant world today there exists a freedom of thought and opinon that is unlimited. Conflicting ideas and theories are allowed full play, and there is an ever-increasing faith that the true idea will win in the end and pass into life and practise.

And Protestantism stands no less for political than for religious freedom. In their formal organization politics and religion are distinct, but the thinking which is characteristic of religious life will pass over into political life. "No bishop, no king," reasoned James I. Freedom claimed and won in the realm of the Church leads legitimately to freedom also in the State; and a democratic Church leads inevitably to a democratic State. But democracy is not simply the demand of each man for self-freedom; it means also his recognition of his neighbor's freedom. A true democracy is, then, a vital outcome of Protestantism, applied or to be applied to every great public human relation.

In our own time the principle is finding its application in the department of industry. The world has become conscious of a new problem in the inequitable distribution of wealth, and seeks a solution of it in various ways. Two typical solutions are offered: the collective ownership and administration of property commonly called socialism, and democracy; and with these are other solutions which combine features of both.

Generally speaking, the Protestant, using this term in its widest sense, believes in democracy applied to industry as well as to Church and State, and, as in these two other departments of public life the foundation of government should be the people, so he wishes to have the people masters in this department also.

He is not, however, satisfied with the collective ownership of property in all forms. He is too much of an individualist for that. He wishes each man to recognize the industrial right of every other man; he wishes each man, at least each able man, to share in the production of wealth, and to share in the results of industrial effort according to his capacity and willingness to work. He will seek his solution of the problem, then, not in taking away property and making it common, but in ensuring as far as possible that wealth shall be used for the common good and that every man who needs work shall have work, and that under the best conditions and with equitable reward. On the other hand, he will not hesitate to ask those whom fortune has favored and law protected in the gaining of wealth, to share, in ways legal and just from the standpoint of the common good, the use of his accumulations with those of his fellows who have been less fortunate. And he will not hesitate to take such control of organized capital as will ensure honest administration and fair treatment for the public. For real freedom, in industry as elsewhere, is the freedom of all. The industrial body, like the body politic, consists of individuals, and is to be conducted for the interests of the individuals who compose it and are to compose it; and the place of each man in the industrial world will be best assured, not by considering first his material needs, but his manhood rights as an industrial unit, which are of far more importance than that he should be comfortably housed, clothed, fed and cared for in his old age. Manhood lives by possession and responsibility. A true industrial environment must furnish him with these, and that not in an indirect or indistinct way, but clearly enough and near enough so that he can see the results of his own efforts. The human personality is the ultimate thing, not the human body, and the character of men comes in for consideration before their comfort. That man will make the best citizen and be the person of truest moral development who can say to society not only, "That is yours," but also, "This is mine." There is something in each man which belongs to his fellows, and there is something which belongs to himself. The proper apportionment of these two properties furnishes the method of democratic government.

The fourth dynamic of Protestantism is the passion for improvement. Were it not for this element, the Reformation, with its strong emphasis on the individual and his rights, would be strangely overbalanced. But as it is, individualism of philosophy is tempered by altruism of practise, and the alloy thus formed is social material of the firmest and most durable. Luther furnishes in himself a fine illustration of this combination. A man of German birth, he had the Teuton's love of freedom, and while a novice in the Augustinian monastery of Erfurt his religious experience took the form of a strong desire to be free from the burden of guilt. He found no relief in the penances and prescribed method of the monastic life. He confided his trouble to the superior of his order, who tried to give a subjective form to his thought and experience, and with some success; but it was not until he found in the writings of Paul the doctrine of justification by faith that he gained full moral freedom and self-mastery. By this experience he gained an impulse toward freedom in other things, and went on step by step, until at last in perfect boldness, he was ready to burn the pope's bull of excommunication which cut him off from the Roman Church. With this experience there had come another no less vital and real. He had encountered the monk Tetzel on his way through Germany shamelessly vending indulgences and deliverances from purgatory, and he had spoken forth with the wrath of condemnation. He had thus become the champion of others, and by so doing had given the cause of the Reformation a nobler objective than that of individual freedom. From that time on it has been, in spite of occasional halts, an organized effort for world improvement. It attempts not only to benefit the individual directly by giving him special rights, but also by making his whole environment the best and fairest possible. Home, church, school, government, business life, international relations, all become objects of championship and improvement. There is nothing in the whole realm of human life but what this spirit of improvement seeks to affect. The forces of individualism are but pioneers for this altruistic attempt at universal righteousness and peace.

It is easy to fall into the argumentation of *post hoc ergo propter hoc*, and this is particularly true in dealing with historic sub-

VIII. The Dynamics Of Protestantism

jects. In trying to trace the historic effects of the Reformation movement allowance must be made for natural development; for the due effect of the New Learning, by itself considered; for the civilizing effect of the Roman Church upon western Europe previous to the time of the Reformation; for the inherent qualities of the Teutonic races; for the discoveries of Columbus and other explorers and the wonderful spell which these cast over the imagination of the people of those days. But when all this has been accounted for, there is left much that would have no explanation were it not for the Reformation.

It is to our purpose to observe that some European nations became Protestant and that some did not, and that some felt the movement more than others. By noting any contrasts that may thus become plain we shall be able to make out more clearly the legitimate results of the Reformation. Great Britain, Holland, Switzerland, Germany and Scandinavia are easily classed as Protestant by virtue of their participation in the reform movement. There is also another nation which in the writer's estimation deserves the name in a large measure, i.e., France. It is true that a large part of the population of France is connected with the Roman Church. But it must be remembered that this country was for a long time debatable ground; that the struggle there was violent, prolonged and widespread, a civil war of religion; that thereby the subjects of Protestant thought became familiar to all the people, and though force of arms and policy of State won the formal victory for Catholicism, the ideas of Protestantism found root in the thinking of the people, and today France, though having so large a proportion Catholic, is in some ways more Protestant than Germany. It seems just to include France within the sway of Protestant influence—it is a democracy; it stands for freedom of thought and the supremacy of reason; furthermore, it has separated Church and State; it is intense in its devotion to truth and is preeminently an intellectual nation among intellectual nations.

Little Switzerland among the mountains, shut in by other nations, was yet in the first century of the Reformation a primal force in the new movement. But as it spread to more populous countries, and to those which had greater natural advantages, the headship of Protestantism was taken away from her. Germany fought the great land battles of the Reformation, and at last with the help of Gustavus Adolphus of Sweden won for Protestantism a sure place in history, while England and Holland for their part wrested the control of the seas from Spain; and France, sympathizing partly with one and partly with the other cause, suffered as much as any nation, and it may be after all, shared as much as any in the Reformation, though but half conscious of it. This group of nations with the United States, the great Protestant nation of America, have come already to be the dominating powers of the world's life. Only since the recent rise of Japan have they had any real rivals except among themselves. Whether from the standpoint of armament, of civilization, or of industry and commerce, their position is an assured one. Russia with its immense territory and millions of population lags behind, having not those social forces which Protestantism provides, and China and India, ancient and populous, look for their inspiration to the later peoples of the Occident? How much has Protestantism to do with this?

We may note first the effort toward popular education and the development of science which is characteristic of Protestant nations. The ideal of improvement is a people generally educated for the double purpose of practical service and the appreciation of life. But it does not stop here; the fuller knowledge of the truth and the deeper mysteries of the world appeal to men of unusual mental power, and lead them to be investigators and interpreters for the rest of mankind; freedom and inspiration

VIII. The Dynamics Of Protestantism

they find in Protestant environment, and their discoveries have introduced a new era in human life. The child is now taught that which was a mystery to the wise man of old, and the common man is the intellectual superior of ancient nobles and kings. We live in a changed world. Telescope, microscope and crucible in the hands of scientifically trained men have opened the windows of truth to us and we look out upon a vast universe of law and order, wisdom and power, wonderful, awe-inspiring, God-revealing. And we observe that the men whose names are great in this department of human effort belong to nations that have felt the impulse of Protestantism.

Along with this development of science goes in a practical way the parallel progress of invention. It would require a volume simply to catalog the useful inventions that have been made since Gutenburg turned off from his type the first printed page of the Bible. Mechanism has changed the whole world of economics, largely altering the form of human society, involving new relations and bringing new conditions. More than this, it has given privileges and comforts to the common people which were once the prerogatives of kings. For a day's wages a man may travel a hundred miles in a finer coach than was ever possessed by a Roman emperor. By careful savings he may build him a house possessing comforts that King Solomon never dreamed of, while for a penny or two the newsboy hands him a paper which tells him more of the world's life than Ben-hadad could learn from a thousand couriers, and the result of a week's labor will purchase more literature than the richest homes possessed in the times of Queen Elizabeth. As we enumerate the more notable of these inventions, the steam engine in all its applications, the dynamo, the telegraph, the telephone, the ocean cable, machinery for textile and other manufacture, we are struck by the fact that these things had their beginnings in Protestant nations.

No less striking is the amelioration which has taken place, and is still taking place, in the social structure of the nations. The Genevan republic of Calvin's time was an anomaly. Today all European nations have their parliaments, even Russia and Turkey. Democracy is to be traced in its progress down the current of history from Geneva to Holland, Scotland, England and America, and thence by example and reaction back to France and the rest of Europe and the world, until in our day it has become the political ideal of all races. But the form of democratic government serves only as an opportunity for the activities of an honest citizenship. A republic cannot be maintained, except in form, unless its common citizens are trustworthy and intelligent. This is the improvement that Protestantism would bring to every nation, that the character of its people should be such as to ensure freedom and fair dealing, without regard to who the rulers may be, or what governmental form they are organized under. This is the real democracy, and there is no other.

One of the noteworthy things of our American republic is the system of credit. An enormous amount of business is done in trust and honestly done. Positions of great authority and trust are filled by men of true patriotism and solid integrity. National interests are jealously guarded, and national reforms bravely and unselfishly led, and in the background is the great body of the people who trust and are trusted. An occasionally discovered culprit in office, an occasional embezzler brought to justice, only serve to call attention to the fact of common honesty among the American people.

Not so distinctive a statement can be made in regard to literature in the highest sense of the word. Yet on this subject there is something to be said. We easily recall such great names as Shakespeare and Milton, but not in these men and their writings do we find the most significant facts. All great eras have had their literary great men. Protestantism has something

VIII. The Dynamics Of Protestantism

which these other movements did not possess—a vast and wonderfully varied literary product which ranks in quality close to the work of genius, not quite possessing such distinctive merit, but having a readability which the products of genius often do not have, and producing a far greater effect because it places in the hands of the people at large the interesting facts of the great world of life and imagination in a form which they can easily understand. Finer literature the Greeks no doubt had, perhaps also the Romans, but such a wealth and variety, such a fountain of helpful and accessible knowledge and sentiment never existed before. The book, the magazine, the newspaper in the hands of the people from infancy fancy to failing age make effective the dream of Calvin, who asked for schools that the common people might be able to read for themselves the words of the sacred Scriptures.

All these great things, however, pale in comparison with the chief characteristic of Protestantism, that wonderful spiritual and moral passion upon which all else depends, that intense longing for the will of God to be done on earth as it is in heaven, which leads men into willing sacrifice and suffering for the sake of others' redemption, and which is the modern counterpart of the passion of Christ and the apostles—the same whether found in Savonarola or Luther, Xavier or Dober, Father Marquette or William Carey.

The supreme concern of real Protestantism is the moral reform and development of mankind. It asks for a personal, vital religious experience in every man, and seeks to call this forth by some form of evangelism. It claims for itself the name "Evangelical," and at home and abroad endeavors to call the attention of men to the heinousness of sin and the glory of the spiritual life. The evangelical teaching was at first misapplied by some who would turn liberty into license, but the personal appeal to men to conform their lives to the gospel teaching met with general response. Results were soon manifest in the change of life and character. Protestants were promptly recognized, and often ridiculed, as possessing to a marked degree an independent moral life. The Lutherans, the Genevese, the Huguenots, the Hollanders, the Scotch Covenanters, the English Puritans won distinction for their moral worth and stability. Before their acceptance of evangelical doctrines and ideals, they were in no way differentiated from their fellows. This result had a definite cause; the demand for a nobler ideal of Christian living brought into existence a new type of manhood. Under this type a man lives a life in which truth is the great authority and love the great fulfilment. He obeys the law, not because he fears the magistrate, but because he sees the reasonableness of so doing. He gives to the Church and for benevolent objects much of his time and money, not under any threat, but out of a sense of duty and service. He lives the moral and religious life, not because Church or custom obliges him to do so, but because he realizes that in so living he is in harmony with the truth of God, and he considers himself not as a man separated from the rest of the world through his spiritual devotion, but rather as an integral part of that life, sharing and partaking in every way with those in the world round about him.

The attempt to improve the Church has resulted most generally in the adoption of some form of autonomy. The Protestant churches are, with the exception of a few State churches, self-managing institutions, independent of the civil government, and with a republican form of government. But the essential thing is not form. The typical Protestant church is a new creation. It begins with the idea that the local church is an association of Christian believers joined together by a covenant of brotherhood and service, and it ends with the conception of the Church as an institution for the moral betterment of humanity through the proclamation of the gospel, its brotherhood life, and the effort to redeem the spiritually unfit. As a local institution, it seeks to be a family of the children of God in which all are equal, except as some are more fit to lead and hold office; but even here the responsibility is diffused among the general membership, and authority exists only as delegated to some of their own number.

As a world organization, it is a spiritual republic made up of smaller bodies federated by a common purpose, and aims at nothing less that the conquest of the whole world for Christ.

The century which saw the first American effort to evangelize the Orient is just now coming to a close. These one hundred years form the most glorious period of modern religious history. The Christ ideal of a world-wide spiritual kingdom has once more been enunciated, and a most noble effort has been made to make that ideal effectual. Consecrated men and women have been sent to every part of the world. Scarce a language now exists into which the story of Christ has not been rendered, and there is no country but feels the force of Christian influence, or in which the nucleus of a native Christian church has not already been formed. Among those who have gone forth under the impulse of this great altruistic movement have been some of the most notable men of modern history, men in character godlike, in moral power heroic, and in effectiveness commanders-in-chief and builders of nations. The faith of these men is magnificent. The daring with which they throw themselves into the conflict is wonderful and their personal effect on the progress of civilization and moral enlightenment ranks them with the great heroes of the Reformation, even with the prophets and apostles. Their power has exceeded that of the armies and navies of the world, their influence is greater than international treaties. They have exhibited in themselves the highest type of manhood, the highest power of moral influence, the most consecrated service. With these spiritual weapons they fight and win.

The gospel of Jesus was inducted into an empire of force, but it was in its essence the contradiction of force. When his over-enthusiastic followers would take him and make him king through force, he repudiated them. He came as the minister of something superior to force, something that in his plan was to take the place of force. Paul puts it into a motto of personal conviction and expression. "The love of Christ constraineth us." The gospel is the substitution of love constraint for force.

The Reformation was the reassertion of this main principle of the gospel. It found the world once again in the clutches of force, and set to work to redeem it. Reason and the moral law the Reformers would substitute for authority and force, duty in place of fear, love in place of law, brotherhood and equality in place of class division and hatred. Men were to be trusted as God's children with the truth of God; as responsible beings they were to be given freedom of thought, of worship, of action; they were to be respected as moral persons, that being respected they might have reason to respond to moral motives and come to rule themselves through the realization of love and duty. Only the man who refused to rule himself should be ruled by force. Force enters not into the life of the man who follows the constraint of love and duty.

But the mission of Protestantism has not yet been fulfilled; it will not be for years to come. The work which the Reformers began we are continuing, and the foundation of universal brotherhood has been laid. The vision of world-wide peace may come to us with greater historic force than it came to the prophet Isaiah, for we can see the beginning of the end. We can see in action everywhere those forces which are to bring about the divine consummation of history, for we hear of those in every nation under heaven who in swiftly increasing numbers have learned with Paul to say and live,

"THE LOVE OF CHRIST CONSTRAINETH US."

www.ingramcontent.com/pod-product-compliance
Lightning Source LLC
Chambersburg PA
CBHW011315080526
44587CB00024B/4009